EXPERIMENTS

with a

MICROSCOPE

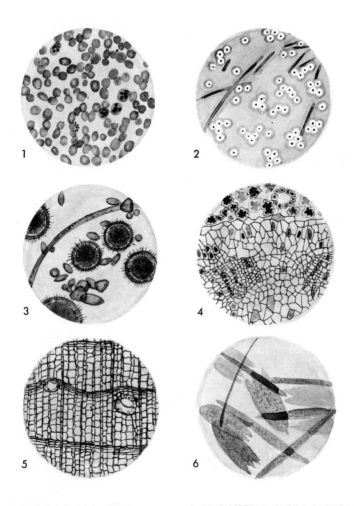

1. HUMAN BLOOD CELLS

2. BREAD MOLD
   MYCELIA AND SPORES

3. VARIOUS POLLEN GRAINS

4. PINE NEEDLE CROSS SECTION

5. WHITE PINE WOOD CELLS

6. SCALES FROM BUTTERFLY'S WING

EXPERIMENTS

with a

MICROSCOPE

Nelson F. Beeler

Franklyn M. Branley

Illustrated by Anne Marie Jauss

$j578$

Thomas Y. Crowell Company · New York

Acknowledgment is made to the following for permission
to reproduce the illustrations on the pages indicated:
Bausch & Lomb Optical Co., pages 22, 25, 66, 67
William P. D. Bush, page 137
General Biological Supply House, adaptations on pages 76, 98, 105
Westinghouse Electric Corporation, pages 99, 148

Library of Congress Catalog Card Number 56-9796

1422679

CONTENTS

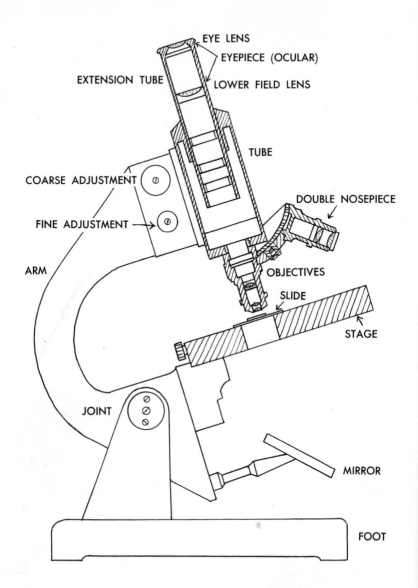

EYE LENS

EYEPIECE (OCULAR)

EXTENSION TUBE

LOWER FIELD LENS

TUBE

COARSE ADJUSTMENT

DOUBLE NOSEPIECE

FINE ADJUSTMENT

ARM

OBJECTIVES

SLIDE

STAGE

JOINT

MIRROR

FOOT

MICROSCOPE (CROSS SECTION)

CHAPTER ONE

Getting to Know
Your Microscope

You WILL find the experiments in this book exciting to carry out if you are able to use a microscope. But first it is important to learn what the parts of the microscope are called and how they work. If you know the correct terminology and the correct way to operate your instrument, you will, of course, be a better technician.

Your instrument is called a compound microscope because it is made up of two lenses instead of one, as in the case of a simple magnifying glass. The lens near the eye is called the ocular, and the one at the other end of the tube is called the objective.

Frequently, microscopes are made so that the objective lens may be removed and another one put into its place, to vary the magnification. One of these objective lenses would be called the low power objective, and the other

1

the high power objective. In some cases, a third objective may be an oil immersion objective. This is used only when very great enlargements are required. The ocular lenses, or eyepieces, are also interchangeable for the same reasons.

In some microscopes the objective lenses are mounted on a rotating nosepiece. There may be two or three lenses mounted on this part of the instrument. It provides a safe place for keeping the lenses when they are not in use. It also provides a convenient method for changing them; turn the nosepiece slightly and a different lens comes into position.

Different lenses change the magnification. The magnifying power of a microscope is determined by multiplying the power of the eyepiece and that of the objective. For example, if the power of the objective is $10\times$ (called "ten power") and that of the ocular is also $10\times$, then the power of the combination is 10 times 10 or 100. This means that the diameter of the object you see is enlarged 100 times. If we used the same objective lens but replaced the ocular with a $15\times$ lens, we then would have an enlargement of 10 times 15 or 150 diameters.

Frequently beginners are interested primarily in making things larger and larger. If they reach 200 diameters, they want to get to 300, and when this is reached they want to go on to 400. However, there is a limit of magnification that is desirable for the amateur.

When you increase magnification, you decrease the area that you can see. This is only reasonable, for you have just so much area for the image. If the magnification is 100 diameters, and the field that you are observing is filled with a specimen, then 100 units can be seen. But if the magnification is 1000 diameters then you can see only 10 of the units in the same area, or one-tenth of the total field. When the field is narrowed in this manner, more precision is required to prepare the specimen and also to handle it properly while it is under the objective. Learn how to use a microscope properly under the low power before you venture into the field of high power magnification.

A proper light supply is as important to good microscopy as the lenses. All that you see under a microscope

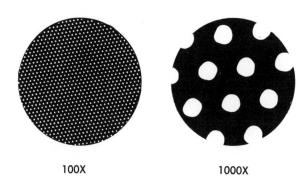

100X   1000X

you see because of light that enters your eye. And the control of that light is vastly important. Your microscope is probably equipped with a movable mirror below the stage, the part on which the slide is mounted. This may be a flat mirror mounted so it can be moved in both a horizontal and vertical plane; or it may be a curved mirror that moves in the same manner. The curved mirror can gather more light. When you rely upon the mirror, you must work in a room where there is adequate lighting, or near a window. If you can afford it, buy an electric substage lamp. It furnishes just the right amount of illumination (so whatever is being observed is seen to best advantage). Or perhaps you might wish to make your own substage lamp as follows:

Cut a two-pound wooden Velveeta cheese box in half and nail the end piece in position so you have a box exactly one half the length of the original. On one side measure down 1 inch from the top of the box and, with this center point, cut a 1½-inch hole with a coping saw. Cover this hole with a piece of translucent plastic or with a piece of frosted glass. (You can frost glass by rubbing together two plates of glass that have a little valve-grinding compound between them.) The plastic or the glass can be glued into position.

Obtain a 2-watt lamp and an electric socket into

which the lamp will fit. Fasten this socket into the base of the box and then cover the box with a sheet of heavy cardboard or a thin piece of wood. Plug the lamp into the house circuit and you will have a source of diffused, soft light. Place the light in front of the mirror that is below the stage of your microscope.

More expensive microscopes are frequently equipped with a substage condenser. This is simply a lens beneath the stage which gathers in light from the mirror and focuses it at the small opening in the stage. A condenser

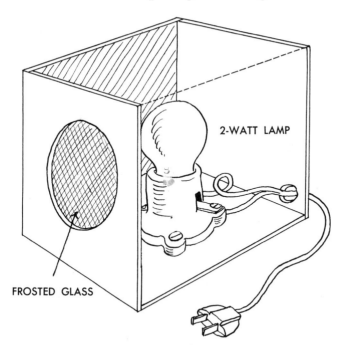

2-WATT LAMP

FROSTED GLASS

usually has an iris diaphragm that can be opened and closed to regulate the amount of light that shines through the slide. As you work with your microscope you will learn what light is needed for different kinds of viewing.

Sometimes it is better to illuminate the slide only from above. This can be done with a flashlight. Or you may wish to experiment with an ordinary reading glass and focus the light of a plain electric light onto the slide. This technique is especially interesting when you are studying living animals that are found in pond water. Put the slide on top of a piece of black paper and shine the light into the drop of water to produce different effects.

Your microscope will probably have two knobs for focusing. One of these is called the coarse adjustment, and the other the fine adjustment. When you are focusing, use the coarse adjustment first and then the fine adjustment to bring the image into a close focus.

Never focus by moving the tube downward, for you may break the slide or scratch the objective. Always move the tube away from the stage. Slip the slide in position under the objective. Watching from the side, move the barrel down so the objective almost touches the slide. Then look through the eyepiece and move the objective away from the slide by using the coarse adjustment knob.

As soon as the specimen comes into view, switch to the fine adjustment knob. Adjust this knob to bring the specimen into sharp focus.

If you plan to spend much time at your microscope, learn to use both eyes. Squinting through one eye is tiring and can cause strain. To train yourself, hold a piece of paper over one eye while viewing. Or better yet, cut out a piece of cardboard about 6 by 3 inches. One inch from an end cut out a hole a trifle smaller in diameter than the barrel of your instrument. Slip this cardboard over the barrel and leave it there so you can never see anything through the eye that is not at the eyepiece, and so your hands will be free to manipulate specimens.

Develop the proper technique for handling specimens under the objective. It is confusing at first to find that when you move the object away from you the image moves toward you, and when you move the object to the right the image moves to the left. Practice a while until

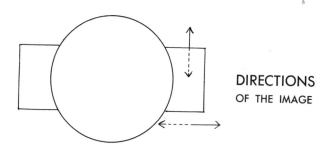

DIRECTIONS
OF THE IMAGE

you are able to move the object correctly the first time. Print a small letter *e* on a piece of paper 1 by 3 inches and place this under the objective. Try to get the letter at the exact center of the field, then move it to the right, the left, up, and down until you can move it precisely and accurately without thinking about it.

Instead of referring to directions as right or left, up or down, microscopists refer to the numbers on the face of a clock. When you are looking through the microscope, your body is at 6:00 o'clock. The direction directly ahead of you is 12:00 o'clock, to your right is 3:00 o'clock, and to your left is 9:00 o'clock. All other directions are based on this clock picture.

Now that you know the various parts of your microscope and some of the basic rules for using it, we shall talk about more interesting things that you can discover.

CHAPTER TWO

How a Microscope Works

O BJECTS FAR away from us appear small, while those close to us appear large. And the closer we are, the more details we can see. A microscope brings us these details.

The effect of distance on the apparent size of an object can easily be proved. Place a water glass 30 feet from you. Hold a pencil upright at arm's length by wrapping four fingers about it, leaving your thumb free. Line up the top of the pencil with the top of the glass. Move your thumbnail along the pencil until it lines up with the bottom of the glass. Measure this length on the pencil and you will find that a glass that is actually 5 inches tall will seem to be only ¼ inch high. As you move closer to the glass, it becomes larger and larger.

If you work this out carefully you will find that the object appears twice as large every time you halve the dis-

9

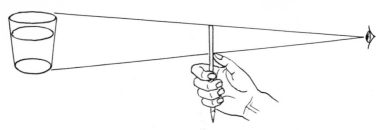

tance. If the glass measures ¼ inch on the pencil at 30 feet, it will measure ½ inch at 15 feet, and so on.

Actually, what happens is that the viewing angle becomes greater as you move closer to the glass. And the greater the viewing angle, the larger the image.

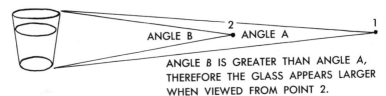

ANGLE B IS GREATER THAN ANGLE A, THEREFORE THE GLASS APPEARS LARGER WHEN VIEWED FROM POINT 2.

While looking at the type in this book, move the book slowly toward your eyes. Stop as soon as the words go out of focus, and measure the distance from your eyes to the book. The distance will vary somewhat from person to person. However, in every case it will be around 3 inches because the normal human eye cannot focus on an object closer to it than that.

Now, if we use a magnifying glass, we can get much closer to an object and still keep a focus. Therefore the object appears larger.

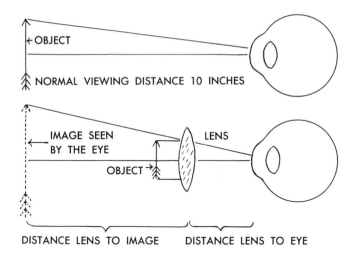

OBJECT

NORMAL VIEWING DISTANCE 10 INCHES

IMAGE SEEN BY THE EYE

LENS

OBJECT

DISTANCE LENS TO IMAGE   DISTANCE LENS TO EYE

Light is bent when it passes through glass at an angle. When the glass is shaped like the lens of a magnifying glass, the light is concentrated at a single point, called the focus. If you place your eye at that focus, objects seen through the glass appear larger than they actually are.

The focus point of a lens can be seen easily. In a darkened room shine a flashlight beam through a reading

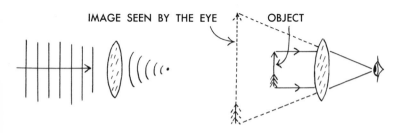

IMAGE SEEN BY THE EYE   OBJECT

glass. Have someone blow a puff of smoke on the oppo-
site side of the lens, and you will see the beam of light
come together, or converge, in a cone. The tip of this
cone is the focus. The distance from the lens to this point
is the focal length of the lens.

Any transparent object, even water, with a smoothly
curved surface may be used as a magnifier. Place a drop
of water on a slide. Hold the slide near the eye and look
through the drop at a specimen, perhaps a fly's wing

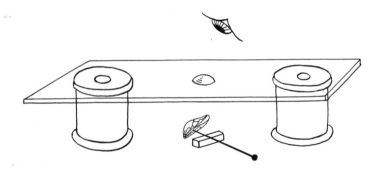

stuck on the end of a needle. You will be surprised at the
amount of enlargement. Frequently the drop is shaken
out of position, so it is better to place the slide on two upright spools. The specimen can then be moved into position without disturbing the drop.

A piece of wire used with a drop of water makes an
even better lens: better because it produces greater mag-

nification and gives a truer picture of the object. Bend a piece of wire around a nail to make a closed loop. Remove the nail. Be sure that the loop is completely closed and as perfectly round as you can make it.

Carefully dip the loop in water. If the loop is well made, it will fill with a spherical drop. The drop will curve equally above and below the wire so that it can be used as a lens with double curvature. Hold the lens near the eye and look at a well-illuminated object—your finger tip, for example. The lines of your fingerprint will show up clearly and look like mountains with valleys between. A simple lens such as this frequently gives magnification of several diameters. A good lens can magnify as much as a hundred times. You will find, however, that the amount of material which the water-drop lens can take in is very limited. We say that it doesn't have a very large field. You will have difficulty, too, maintaining the lens and the specimen and the eye at the proper distances from each other. You can make a handier water-drop magnifier from a strip of tin can. Cut a strip of tin 1 inch wide and 4 inches long from a tin can. File and snip off the sharp edges so that there is no danger of being cut. Place the center of the tin strip over a wood block— preferably hardwood—and make a hole in the center of the strip with a small finishing nail. Turn the strip over

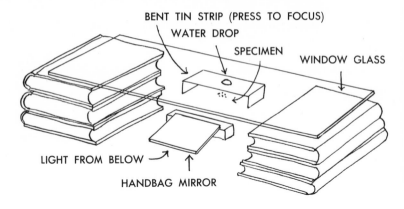

BENT TIN STRIP (PRESS TO FOCUS)
WATER DROP
SPECIMEN
WINDOW GLASS
LIGHT FROM BELOW
HANDBAG MIRROR

and file off the burr made by the nail. Drive the nail through the metal from this side and turn it around several times to make the hole as nearly round as possible.

Bend down the tin about ¼ inch from each end. Set up a piece of window glass between books as shown in the illustration. Place the bent tin on it. Set a small handbag mirror directly beneath the tin. Tilt the mirror at an angle with a book or block of wood.

Dip a toothpick in water. Carefully remove it and allow the drop of water it carries to fall into the hole in the tin. With a little practice you can form a perfectly round drop which bumps up as far above the tin as it hangs down below.

Place a few grains of salt or some fine thread on the window glass beneath the droplet for your first specimen. Adjust the mirror so that light is reflected up

14

through the salt to the water-drop lens. Focus the lens, if necessary, by pressing lightly on the tin.

The water drop will eventually evaporate and it will have to be replaced. But water drops are cheap. However, a drop of glycerine will not evaporate and gives a better magnification. You will need to place your eye quite near the lens as you did with the wire loop lens. Leeuwenhoek, the inventor of the microscope, made some amazing discoveries with a magnifier no better than this. Unfortunately, once in a while he also saw some things that weren't there.

If you rub the hole with a little Vaseline, removing the excess with a cloth, the drops will be rounder. The water cannot wet the tin because of the thin film of oil. Thus it cannot flow away but must remain bumped up in the lens shape we want. Wiping the tin with a piece of the silicone-treated paper used for eyeglass lenses will do the same thing.

This water-drop magnifier has one decided advantage over the droplet on a wire loop, or the half drop on a slide: the object you are examining is illuminated from behind. The light moves through the specimen just as it does in the compound microscope. In the other devices the light must be reflected from the specimen and hence cannot be made as bright. You will find that proper lighting is one of the most difficult arrangements to make with any microscope, simple or compound.

Another difficulty involves focal length. Focal length is the distance between the center of a lens and the point where light is brought to a focus. You saw this in the experiment of shining a beam through a reading glass in a dark room, mentioned earlier in the chapter.

If an object is a little beyond the focal length of a lens, the image formed on the other side will be enlarged. This

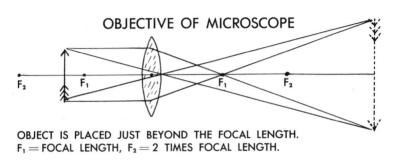

OBJECTIVE OF MICROSCOPE

OBJECT IS PLACED JUST BEYOND THE FOCAL LENGTH.
F_1 = FOCAL LENGTH, F_2 = 2 TIMES FOCAL LENGTH.

is the way the light is controlled in an ordinary projector. And it is the way it is controlled in a microscope. The object is placed just a little beyond the focal length of the objective lens. An enlarged image of the object is formed inside the tube, and the ocular lens makes an enlargement of the image.

To see how this works, light a candle in a darkened room. Hold a reading glass upright in one hand and a

16

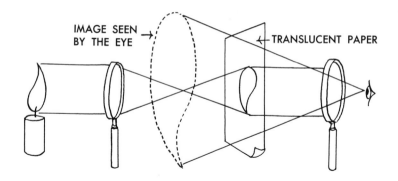

IMAGE SEEN BY THE EYE →

← TRANSLUCENT PAPER

vertical sheet of thin paper in the other hand. Focus the image of the candle flame on the paper.

Have someone else focus on this image from the other side of the paper with another reading glass. Now remove the paper, and the second person will see a much enlarged image of the candle flame. The image may be so large that he can see only part of the flame.

You have made a basic microscope but it could have been improved by having for your objective a lens with a very short focal length (so you could get closer to the candle).

Light is made of many different wave lengths, the longest of which produces the color red, and the shortest, violet. Simple lenses do not bend all of the wave lengths to the same degree, therefore the various waves are not brought to the same focus. The observer using such a lens will see a blurred image, with bands of color at the edges.

17

To correct this condition lenses are made of different kinds of glass cemented together. One kind of glass might control the red waves, and another the violet, so all of the wave lengths are brought to a focus. Therefore the lenses in microscopes must be well made. The glass must be without flaws, and it must be color corrected. Lenses in good instruments are achromatic, which means that color fringes will not form around the edges.

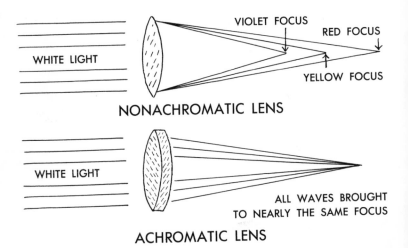

NONACHROMATIC LENS

ACHROMATIC LENS

CHAPTER THREE

Let's Look at Something

WE HAVE eyes to see with, yet we see very little of the fascinating world all about us. Now that you have a microscope, new vistas are opened to you. You will see things you never knew existed, and many common things you have seen every day of your life will take on a new excitement. In many cases this new insight will be an improvement over the old; it will make things look better than they did before and it will help you understand why things behave as they do. In other instances the new insight will be a disappointment. For many of the things we think we know about are really much different when we view them up close. We have become used to the ideas we have formed from a distance and we like them; the microscope gives us a ringside view and sometimes this is disappointing. But all knowledge may be turned to

19

some use, and what we learn through our microscope may be of the greatest value to us someday.

You have learned how to handle your microscope in the previous chapters. You have some idea of how and why it operates. Now look at some of the everyday things that are before you. In all of the work suggested in this chapter, use the lowest power of your microscope to begin with. This will make locating the images easier for you and it will also make it possible for you to see a larger field. Many people use high power too often. You get a larger magnification, it is true, but frequently you lose the chance to see things in proper relationship to other things in the specimen.

Pick up a newspaper photograph. The picture looks smooth and regular to the naked eye. Actually it is far from smooth and regular. If you look at the picture with a magnifying glass, an ordinary reading glass, you will see that what you thought was a smooth, black surface is only a series of black dots separated by white spaces. If you look at a section of the picture under the low power of your microscope, the dots are seen to be irregular smudges. Look at a black and white illustration taken from a "slick" paper magazine. The same dotted pattern will appear. However, the dots will be more regular in shape and there will be more of them in any given area.

20

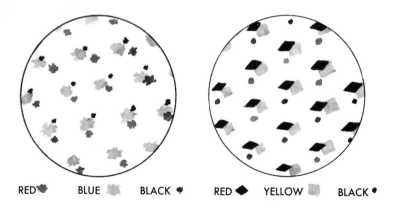

RED ●   BLUE ●   BLACK ●   RED ◆   YELLOW ●   BLACK ●

Look at a dark part of the picture and at a lighter part. Are the dots all the same size? Is the dark part of the picture made of blacker dots or are they merely closer together? Are some parts made of white dots on a black background? What can you tell about the way the ink acts on the paper? If you were to compare the action of ink on newspaper stock and on slick paper, what would you say? If you were a tiny bug creeping over the paper, what would you report that you had "seen" when you got home to your family?

Newspaper pictures are made with dots about 60 to the inch. The finest pictures in expensive books are made with as many as 400 to the inch. Compare a printed picture with a snapshot or photograph. The gradations of light and dark are more gradual. They are made of tiny bits of metallic silver imbedded in the shiny coat of the photograph paper. These bits are too small for the micro-scope to detect as individual pieces. That is why the real picture seems so much sharper than the printed one. An aerial photograph is even more interesting to study. You may be able to get a whole tree or a whole house under the microscope and actually tell what it is. You can pick out windows on a house that may have been miles away in the original scene.

The letters of a typewriter make distinct impressions. They are so different that a skilled observer can tell ac-curately whether a letter was written with a particular machine. Studying the impressions made by two or more machines to see the variations shows how carefully a detective must work.

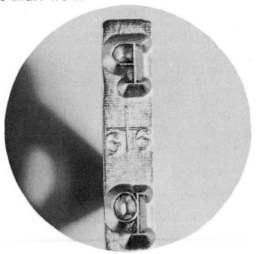

Color pictures show up in an even more startling fashion. If you look at a colored picture post card, first with a magnifying glass and then with the low power of your microscope, you will see a smooth, filmy cloud made up of black, blue, and yellow dots. Some of the yellow dots are separated entirely from the blue ones, while others overlap the blue. When viewed by the unaided eye the dots blend together to make a smooth gradation of color. When viewed through the microscope, the picture is a meaningless jumble of irregular splotches of individual colors. Look at various colors on the card to determine how they are made up. On our picture post card we found that a brownish, rocky ledge was made of a multitude of red, green, and black dots on a yellow field. We also looked at color print in a slick paper magazine and found that a picture of the surface of a planet which appeared pink was actually made of diamond-shaped splotches of red ink, covered here and there by square yellow splotches. Small round black dots were scattered over the surface.

Indeed, things are not always what they seem; lovely colored pictures that are a pleasure to look at are, in reality, simply organizations of dots of colors which, by themselves, mean nothing.

In this chapter we are concerned with looking at things

just to get some idea of what we have been missing. Let us do a bit of snooping to find other possibilities. Suppose we tear a piece of paper and put the torn edge under the microscope. When you observe the edge of the paper, try different sources of illumination: the light might come from beneath the stage in the traditional manner, or it might come from above the object. You can light it from above by holding a flashlight so the beam of light falls upon the paper, or adjust a table lamp so it shines directly down on the specimen. You are in for a surprise because what appeared to the unaided eye to be a smooth tear is actually so uneven that it looks like an impassable tangle of coarse swamp grasses growing in every direction and in all sorts of thicknesses and configurations. Tear a piece of newspaper and look at it. Compare this with a good grade of writing paper, with a piece of hard finish bond, and with a piece of cleaning tissue, and notice the differences.

The principle behind another sort of detective work can be seen by examining the cutting edge of a razor blade. Compare the edge of a used blade with a brand new one. You will see why your father discarded the old blade. This is another situation where top or side lighting may give better results than lighting from underneath the object. Police use this system when comparing

24

bullets, one from the victim and one from the suspected gun. Very tiny scratches and marks are made on the bullet when it is fired from a particular gun. The microscope shows them up just as it shows the fine markings on a razor blade.

The world is yours for observing. Once you start, there s no stopping place, for almost everything has secrets hat the microscope will reveal—for instance, the filanent from an electric light bulb. Place an old bulb in a heavy paper or cloth bag. Smash the bulb with a hammer. You are in for a surprise when you look at a bit of the filament under your microscope.

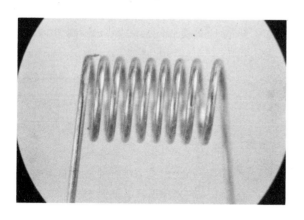

Try grains of sand and crystals of salt and sugar. Crystals should be placed on a slide and the glass placed under the microscope. Look at the crystals when the

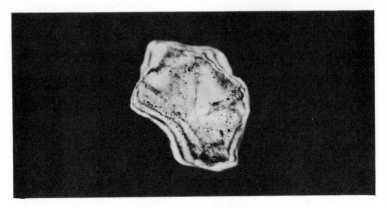

GRAIN OF SAND

light comes from beneath them. Then slip a piece of black paper beneath the crystals, light them from the side, and they look like a collection of jewels, catching the light and sometimes dispersing it to produce the colors of the rainbow.

The refrigerator is a treasure house of materials for observation. Look at the leaves of carrot and celery, bits of lettuce, a speck of egg white, the inner membrane separating the egg from the shell, some of the ice scraped from the cooling coils, a speck of mayonnaise or French dressing.

Look at coffee, oatmeal, or spices in the kitchen cabinet. Try pepper, celery seed, oregano, bay leaves. There are lots of surprises awaiting you.

Cut open a potato. Scrape off a bit of the flesh of the

potato or cut a paper-thin slice with a razor blade. Place the slice or pulp on a slide. Adjust the light to reduce glare and you will see cells of the potato. To make the cells stand out and to show the part of the cell that contains starch, you can stain the potato on the slide. Mix about ten drops of tincture of iodine from the medicine cabinet in a teaspoonful of water. Place a drop of the solution on the potato with a medicine dropper. Tilt the slide so the excess solution runs off. Then examine the potato. The cells will now show blue-black sections in the regions where starch is concentrated. Later in the book you will find a whole chapter on staining. This technique is especially valuable for improving our knowledge of what is beneath the microscope lens.

Onion skin cells show up very clearly under the microscope and they can be stained effectively. Remove the outer covering of an onion and cut off the top. The cross section you have exposed is made up of layers. Each of the layers is separated from the next one by a very thin membrane. This is called onion skin. (It is the reason why very thin typing paper is sometimes called onionskin.) Remove a layer of the onion and then carefully peel off a piece of the membrane. Under the microscope you will see that the skin is made of a multitude of small cells like little boxes. These cells are easier to see if you color them.

Use ordinary permanent blue fountain pen ink. Allow the ink to stay on the onion skin for a short time. Wash off the excess with tap water. Now compare the appearance of the skin with the original unstained specimen.

Another interesting specimen is a scale from a fish. Just place a scale on a slide and examine it under the microscope. If the scale is illuminated from above, you will see a multitude of iridescent colors; colors that change constantly with each small shift you make in the angle of the light beam.

Put a pearl button under the microscope. Light it from the side. Focus on a part of the button which seems to show color. You may be surprised to find no color through the microscope at all. The color appears because of the many closely lined edges of the layers of the oyster shell from which the button was made. As the oyster grew, it deposited a thin layer of shell at a time. The button was stamped out of such a shell, exposing the edges of these very thin layers. They are so tiny that they break up light which strikes them and return only some of the waves to your eyes. This is true also of the coloring of birds. If you look at a pigeon or starling feather, you will see that the bronze color is due to the very fine lines of the feather and not to a pigment.

You can have a long session at the microscope, too, examining a dollar bill. See how carefully the engraving is done. Look for silk threads that are always a part of the paper from which official currency is made.

Anyone who owns a microscope is fortunate indeed. He can search out many possibilities and find how things are actually made. Particles of dust, bits of rock, particles of fingernail, a human hair, an iron filing, sawdust—the world is his to look at and to wonder about. There are a great many "tricks of the trade" for the expert microscopist. (Did you know that's what you are?) But at first he wants only to look at things from the world around him, to see them with his "new eyes" and to marvel.

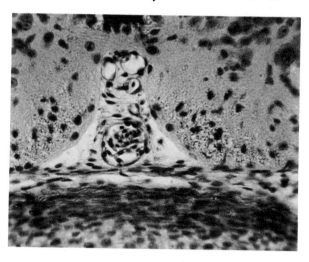

HAIR FOLLICLE
magnified approximately 430x

CHAPTER FOUR

Your First Mounts

IN CHAPTER 3 there are some suggestions for interesting things to look at through your microscope. You are not limited to these suggestions, of course. You have probably already seen many, many more objects than those mentioned.

Often the things you look at are so interesting or unusual that you want to save them to look at later or to compare with new discoveries. In order to do this, you need to mount the specimen you are studying to protect and preserve it. There are a number of problems connected with preserving specimens for the microscope. This chapter will tell you how some of these problems have been solved.

Start with a collection of the glass blanks called slides and the thinner glass pieces called cover glasses or cover slips. The slides are always made of glass but the cover slips are available in unbreakable plastic. Glass cover slips are so thin that it is quite a job to clean them without breaking them. These pieces of equipment are inexpensive so it is best to buy a supply rather than try to reuse them.

Both slides and cover slips must be clean and free from lint. Wash them with a household detergent, rinse them thoroughly with distilled water if possible, and allow them to dry by standing on edge. If you do wipe them dry, use a cloth that has been washed many times so it is free of lint. Rub the glass carefully so no lint is left. A final wiping with lens paper will give you a perfect slide for a mount.

Let us try a fly's wing for our first specimen. In addition to the slide and covers, you will need a pair of tweezers, Canada balsam, and xylol. Canada balsam is a mounting cement that is ideal for microscopic work because it is a liquid that is easy to apply to the object and fluid enough to wet it thoroughly. It is not poisonous to the object. It hardens rapidly at ordinary temperatures. It remains unchanged after it has hardened. It allows light through in just the same way glass does. It is transparent and has very little color. There is an easily obtained solvent (xylol) which can be used to thin it and to remove excess from slides—and from the technician.

There are very few materials that have all these properties.

With tweezers remove a wing from a dead fly. Place the wing at the center of the slide or a little to one side of the center. Place on the wing a drop of Canada balsam. If you have no balsam you can substitute a small drop of clear nail polish or clear household cement of the lacquer type. Balsam is the best cement, however.

Pick up a clean cover glass with forceps or tweezers and place it carefully on the drop, lowering it from one edge so no air bubble is trapped. Press the slip carefully down on the droplet so you do not crush the specimen, using only enough pressure to obtain good contact and remove the air bubbles. If any bubbles are left, they will get in the way when you are looking at the specimen later. They have a way of settling over the exact spot you want to examine!

Bubbles get into the balsam if it is stirred. Always be sure to allow only a clear, bubble-free drop to fall on the specimen and save yourself trouble. With care, a bubble may be pressed to the edge of the cover slip and squeezed out. You must be careful not to squeeze out too much balsam in the process. Enough balsam should be used to produce a thin ring all around the outside edge of the slip.

Don't worry about this excess balsam. After the gum has hardened, the rim of extra balsam can be neatly removed with a little xylol on a piece of lens paper or paper toweling. The finished slide should have no extra balsam visible, so that the cover slip appears smooth all around. Do not drown the slide in xylol, or the solvent will dissolve its way under the edge of the slip. Use just enough to remove the ring of balsam and no more. This takes a little practice but it is a valuable technique to learn. A good technician is known by the appearance of his mounts.

Occasionally you may want to make slides of insect or flower parts that would be damaged if they were pushed down flat under a tight-fitting cover. To avoid crushing a specimen, use a small washer. This can be cut out of cardboard as shown in the illustration. Cement the washer to the slide with balsam or household cement and place the specimen in the hole in the washer. The cover glass is then cemented to the washer. A deeper hole, or well, can be made by cementing two or more cardboard washers together.

For thin specimens a shallower well is better. A thickness of shellac, painted in a circle directly on the slide, will form a shallow well. You may paint this freehand. Or you may fasten a slide to the end of a dowel or an un-

CUT A PIECE OF CARDBOARD THE SAME SIZE AS A SLIDE.

CUT SLIDE-SIZED CARDBOARD INTO THREE PIECES. CUT HOLE IN EACH A LITTLE SMALLER THAN A COVER SLIP.

CEMENT CARDBOARD "WASHER" TO SLIDE.

sharpened pencil with a drop of balsam. After the balsam sets, the whole slide may be rotated by spinning the dowel between the thumb and fingers of one hand. Take a small, fine brush in the other hand, dip it in shellac, and paint a circle of shellac on the other side of the slide by holding the brush still and turning the slide. This technique makes a more workmanlike slide. Frequently one layer of shellac will make a well deep enough for your purpose. If a deeper well is wanted, let the shellac dry and then put on another layer. Loosen the dowel with xylol.

In order to see many cell structures, it is necessary to

have thin sections of plant stems, leaves, roots, and other specimens. A sharp razor blade, preferably single-edged, is essential. If you have only double-edged ones, cover one edge with adhesive tape to keep from cutting yourself.

Hold the stem snugly against a flat surface and you can cut fairly thin sections easily with a little practice.

Many things you want to section, however, collapse as they are cut. The specimen will hold up to be cut more easily if it is embedded in paraffin. Melt some paraffin wax (the kind that is used to cover jelly in glass jars) in a tin can. Let the wax cool somewhat. Just before it has set, dip the stem (or other specimen) into the paraffin. Remove the specimen, allow the paraffin on it to harden and then dip it again. Continue in this way until a wall of paraffin has been formed around the specimen.

Because the specimen has a wall of paraffin around it, it will not collapse when it is cut; and the section, once cut, will be supported by the paraffin so that it will not fold over. Discard the first slice and use the next one.

The laboratory technician cuts extremely thin sections with a device called a microtome. This instrument forces a wax-embedded specimen out of a tube a very, very little at a time. An extremely sharp knife then cuts off the section.

35

To make a simple but effective microtome, get a fine-threaded bolt from the hardware store and a nut to fit. If you rummage around in the box of cast-off nails, screws, and bolts in your cellar, you may find one that will do. Dip a plant stem into paraffin until the stem and paraffin together are about the diameter of the bolt. Put the nut on the end of the bolt. Turn it down two or three threads. Heat the nut gently over a candle flame just enough to warm it. Push the specimen encased in paraffin into the hollow of the nut above the end of the bolt.

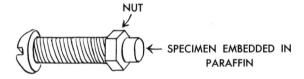

NUT

← SPECIMEN EMBEDDED IN PARAFFIN

FINE-THREADED BOLT

Cut along the face of the nut to square off the specimen. Tighten the nut a quarter of a turn or so. This will force out the specimen a short way. Make another cut along the face of the nut. This will give you a thin section of the plant stem. If this section is placed in water, it will float. When you are ready to use it, the paraffin will flake off and you will have a splendid cross section, thin enough for light to come through easily and thus reveal the cell structure.

To mount the specimen, grasp a cover slip with tweezers and place it in the water under the floating section. Lift the cover slip gently and pick up the section on it. Place the cover glass, specimen side up, on a blotter; and place the glass slide on top. Usually there is enough water left on the cover slip to serve as a bond that will hold the slip to the slide. Grasp the slide by its two ends and turn it over with a quick single motion. Excess water can be removed from the slide with the corner of a blotter or a tiny piece of paper towel.

In hospital laboratories, sections of human tissue must be examined frequently. Cancer, in particular, can be found only when cells from the suspected cancerous growth can be examined under the microscope. The doctor snips a tiny bit of tissue from the patient. This is placed on a microtome equipped with a tank of carbon dioxide gas. When the tank is opened, the gas rushes out quickly and cools the surroundings. In fact, it becomes "dry ice" with a temperature of about —175 degrees Fahrenheit. This freezes the tissue very quickly—so quickly that the water in the cells does not have time to form large ice crystals. Large crystals would pierce the cell walls and destroy them. This would let out the fluid from inside the cells. These "frozen sections" look as nearly like the live cells as it is possible to get them.

A second way to use your homemade microtome is to fill the space between the nut and the bolt with molten paraffin. Before it sets, drop in a small piece of the material you want to section. Microtome it when the wax is cool and hard.

Specimens prepared by a simple dipping in paraffin still contain water in their cells. This water contains the nutrients that kept the cells alive. But as soon as a plant is removed from the soil, the water begins to leave through the cell walls, which are very soft and porous. Look at a thin section of crisp lettuce through your microscope. Compare it with a section of wilted lettuce. Notice how the cells of the crisp lettuce are fat and full of water. The cells of the wilted lettuce have collapsed.

You want your mounted specimens to maintain their original shape. Alcohol will remove the water (and prevent decay) and at the same time strengthen the cell walls.

Water and alcohol will dissolve in each other in all proportions. You can have a 1 per cent water and 99 per cent alcohol solution or the other way around or any percentage combination in between. Water with alcohol in it can pass through cell walls just as pure water can. Alcohol has a property unlike water, though. It will harden cell walls. If you dipped our specimen into very concentrated alcohol, the cell walls would become hardened and be almost like little leather boxes. The water would still remain inside and the inside of the cell would change in appearance. It would begin to decay.

If you put the specimen into a solution of a little alcohol and a lot of water, some alcohol will enter the cell and take the place of the water. The cell still remains fat and full. Now, let us say that you place the specimen in an alcohol-water mixture containing more alcohol. The inside of the cell will soon have less water and more alcohol. If you continue to treat the specimen with more and more concentrated alcohol solutions, the cell will be filled with more alcohol than water. Eventually you will be dunking the specimen into a solution that will harden the cell wall. Up to this point, though, the cell will still have its original shape. Now you can take the tissue from the alcohol bath. The excess alcohol can evaporate but the cell does not collapse because its walls are hardened. You can keep the specimen now. It will not decay. But it looks nearly the same as it did when it was alive. What you have done is to keep the cell filled with a solution until the cell wall hardened. This prevents the collapse of the cell as the water is gradually removed and substituted with alcohol. Any kind of cell, plant or animal, may be treated this way. This process is called fixing.

The best alcohol to use for fixing is ethyl alcohol but this is expensive. There is a large tax on ethyl alcohol because people drink it. Isopropyl alcohol can be used. This can be obtained from a drugstore as almost 100 per cent alcohol. That is, there is very little water mixed with it. You will need only a little—three or four ounces —for your first microscope work.

A handy specimen to begin with is a small insect or insect part. Put four glass slides on the table in front of you. Put 3 drops of distilled water and 1 drop of alcohol on one of the slides. The water and alcohol will mix at once. With tweezers carefully place the insect in this solution. On the second slide place 2 drops of water and 2 of alcohol. Transfer the insect to this after it has been 10 minutes or more in the first one. Make the third solution of 1 drop of water and 3 of alcohol. The insect

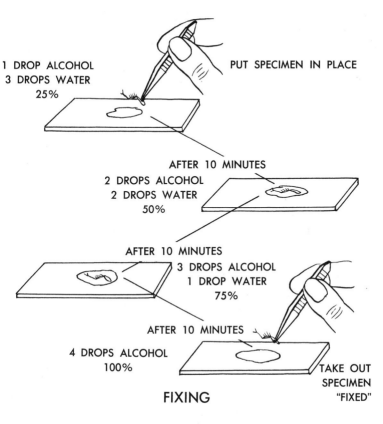

1 DROP ALCOHOL
3 DROPS WATER
25%

PUT SPECIMEN IN PLACE

AFTER 10 MINUTES
2 DROPS ALCOHOL
2 DROPS WATER
50%

AFTER 10 MINUTES
3 DROPS ALCOHOL
1 DROP WATER
75%

AFTER 10 MINUTES
4 DROPS ALCOHOL
100%

TAKE OUT
SPECIMEN
"FIXED"

FIXING

should be placed in this for 10 minutes, also. The fourth slide, of course, has 4 drops of alcohol only. Remove the insect after 10 minutes in the last bath and allow it to dry on a blotter. Mount this specimen in a shallow well with a drop of balsam. Mount a second similar but untreated specimen on another slide. Compare the appearance of the two.

41

Record the time and date when you prepared the slides. Examine them again several days later. Are there now marked differences between them? Indicate under "Remarks" on your record what you think is the cause of the differences if there are any. This careful recording and thinking about what you see through your microscope is one of the parts of the process we call scientific investigation. Examine an unmounted specimen similar to the one you have mounted. Record any differences you see. Try to account for these differences.

Alcohol is very effective in killing bacteria. Bacteria are single cells. The doctor washes the area around a wound with a little alcohol on a piece of cotton. He does not use 100 per cent alcohol, although you might think that the stronger the alcohol the better it would destroy the germs. He uses 70 per cent alcohol usually, because the germ-killing property of alcohol is greatest at this concentration.

A collection of slides carefully recorded will be a source of new ideas of what to try next with your microscope.

In order to keep track of the slides you make you will need to mark them in some way. A small square of gummed paper can be stuck to each slide. This can be labeled with a pencil or a pen. If you have Canada balsam and some xylol, you can arrange to write directly on the slide. Thin the balsam down with xylol until the mixture dries almost as soon as it is put on the slide. Testing will show you the right proportions. Paint some on one end of the slide and allow it to dry. Write directly on this film. Cover the writing with a second layer of thinned-down balsam and you will have a permanent record. The marks now can't slip off as they can with gummed paper. They never get dirty. Wash out the brush in clear xylol before you put it away.

CHAPTER FIVE

The Problem
of Bending Light

WHEN YOU examined onion skin as suggested in chapter 3, you encountered one of the common problems of microscope work. Let us look at it more closely. Place a piece of onion skin on a slide and put a cover slip on to keep it flat. Examine the skin under the microscope. Put a second piece of onion skin on another slide. Place a drop of water on it. Drop a cover slip on top. The water will flatten out under the slip. In fact, the slip will float on a thin, uniform film of water. Examine this piece of onion skin. Note how much clearer the cells appear. The very thin film of water makes a tremendous difference in how well the microscope works.

Let's see why this is so. You see the onion cells by means of the light that comes through them. The light comes from the mirror under the stage on which the specimen is placed. It must move up through the glass slide, then through the onion skin or the air around it. Next it continues through the glass of the cover slip. Then it moves into air. Finally it enters the lens of the microscope. Light bends a little as it moves from glass to air and from air to glass again. Instead of coming straight through the slide-air-cover-slip combination, it zigzags. Some of it escapes and does not enter the tube of the microscope at all.

Light moves through water in much the same way that it moves through glass. When you put a drop of water between the slide and the cover slip, a ray of light moves from glass to water and to glass again. It is bent very little when it goes from one of the materials to another and little of it escapes. As a result, the things we look at have sharp, clear images. They appear brighter too.

Microscopes like the one your doctor uses magnify as much as a thousand times. With one of these it is necessary to connect the top of the cover glass and the objective of the microscope with a liquid. This cuts down the wandering of the light as it leaves the cover slip, enters the air, and moves on into the lens. The liquid used is cedarwood oil. Lenses that are made to be used this way are called oil immersion lenses. Such a lens may cost two or three times as much as your whole microscope.

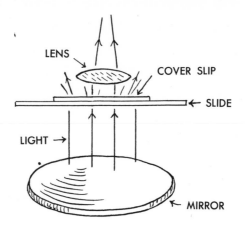

LENS
COVER SLIP
SLIDE
LIGHT →
MIRROR

When you get your first expensive microscope, you will find a small bottle of immersion oil in the case.

Temporary mounts in water dry out very quickly. If you ever get a particularly interesting one that you want to keep for a longer time, touch your finger to some Vaseline and run a thin film of it around the edge of the cover slip. Be sure that you put it over the edge of the cover slip and onto the glass slide. The petroleum jelly makes an airtight seal and the mounts can be kept several days.

The onion skin will die eventually and it will look much different. To keep it alive longer, you can use mineral oil because it is not poisonous to onion cells, nor does it evaporate as water does. Put a drop of this clear, colorless oil on the specimen. Cap it with a cover glass.

You can keep onion skin alive and unchanged four or five days in this kind of mount. The oil is even more like glass in its light-bending properties than water is. Oil is used for expensive microscope work for this reason. Examine and compare a dry mount, a water mount, and a mineral-oil mount of onion skin. Record what you find. Make a note of the reason for the difference in your record book as explained in chapter 7.

The chapter on molds in this book suggests that you mount mold specimens in alcohol and water mixed half and half. There is a reason for this, just as there is a reason for every trick in using the microscope. Scrape a little of the grayish, fluffy stuff from a piece of moldy bread or fruit skin. Place a bit on a slide and cover it with a slip. Mount a second piece in water. Cover a third specimen with one drop of alcohol and one drop of water before putting on the cover. Examine all three.

Note that the one in water is more difficult to see than the one mounted dry. The one in alcohol shows up sharp and clear. The filaments of the mold can be examined easily in an alcohol mount. The reason, strangely enough, is that water is not wet enough for this job. The mold filaments carry a thin film of air around them and the water cannot penetrate the film. The alcohol solution is "wetter" than water. That is, it flows better; it can penetrate the air film around the mold and coat the filaments entirely with liquid. The light does not have to go through air. It travels through liquid only and therefore is not bent very much. In the water mount, the light must travel through water and air, which makes it bend so much that it is practically impossible to see the filaments at all. This is why air bubbles in Canada balsam or other mounting cements are so troublesome.

It is apparent from this chapter that you don't need expensive equipment to learn a lot about how to handle a microscope. Leeuwenhoek, the inventor of the microscope, could learn more from what he saw through a lens made of a single drop of water than many college students learn with an oil immersion instrument costing hundreds of dollars. The techniques that you learn with your cheaper microscope are the same as those that you will need later when you graduate to a three-hundred-dollar instrument. In fact, you will handle an expensive instrument with much more pleasure and profit because of the work you are doing now. It's how you use the instrument that counts!

CHAPTER SIX

Pipes Passing Through Plants

THE STEMS of plants contain a number of pipes, some of which carry soil water up to the leaves. Some of them carry food that has been made in the leaves down to the roots and other parts of the stem. The "strings" in celery are bundles of pipes that go from the roots to the leaves.

Cut a piece about a half inch long from the end of a stalk of celery. After standing it in ink for a minute or so, take it out and wipe off the excess ink. Several dark spots will be visible at the upper end of the piece and dark streaks will show along the edge. These are the strings in the celery, which have picked up ink. The cells surrounding them have hardly any color at all. Cut a thin section from the end of the stalk with a razor blade. Place it on a slide and examine one of the dark spots. You will find that it actually consists of a central collection of ten or more pipes and a crescent of smaller ones. The cells

49

surrounding the pipe ends appear entirely colorless under the microscope. This is because they have taken no ink in through their walls. They look slightly blue to the unaided eye because of the ink on the outside of the cells.

All species of stemmed plants have a characteristic pattern in which these bundles are placed. Sometimes the arrangements take on the appearance of a comical face. The illustration shows how corn plant bundles look. Do the patterns remind you of anyone you know?

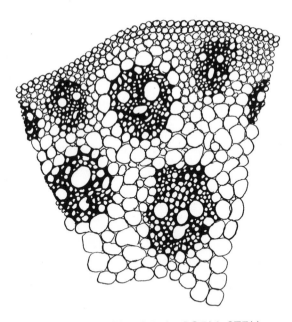

CROSS SECTION OF A CORN STEM

When a plant is alive, the pipes draw in great quantities of soil water all during the day. Much of this water goes to the leaves and is given off to the air. A tree gives off tons of water in a week. You can use your microscope to watch the water streaming into the bottom ends of the pipes.

Beans are a quick-growing plant which you will frequently use in your microscope research. Like most laboratory technicians, you might just as well grow your own. Pin four dried beans (seed beans from the local garden shop) to a piece of cardboard 2 by 3 inches. Place the cardboard in a tumbler containing 2 tablespoonfuls of tap water. Cover with a saucer and place it in a warm spot (not bright and sunny). In two days, growth will have started, and in four or five days the beans will have well-developed leaves.

To carry out your experiment with the plants, buy a Syracuse watch glass in a drugstore for a few cents. Fill it half full of water and add 3 drops of India ink. Put this on the microscope stage under the low power lens.

Cut the bean plant off near the roots. Put the upper end of the stem in water for a few minutes to allow the pipes to fill. Keeping the end of the stem under water, cut off a slice about 2 inches from the end. Cut this at a slant so that a large section of the interior of the stem is

51

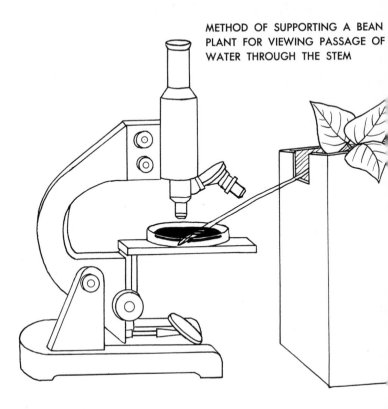

visible. Place the remaining stem in the watch glass with the cut side facing up. The plant can be supported by books or a cardboard carton as shown in the illustration. The cut portion will stay stationary under the lens.

Focus the low power objective on one of the bundles of water-conducting pipes. Watch for streams of water carrying the India ink into the pipes. India ink is made of very, very small carbon particles suspended in water.

52

PIPES PASSING THROUGH PLANTS

Ordinary ink will not do for the observation. Turn the microscope mirror so the field is lighted from an angle and the streams will show up more clearly. After a time the conducting pipes become very dark from the carbon bits they have picked up. They may eventually become plugged and streaming will cease. But the amount of activity in the watch glass during the time the plant is drawing up water is truly amazing.

The water that enters the bottom of the tubes is being given off through the leaves. With your microscope you can look in on the operation of this end of the water-conducting system too. Water goes out of the plant through openings in the underside of the leaves. These openings are called stomata. A single one is a stoma, which means "mouth" in Greek. The stomata are ringed by cells which can swell up or shrink and thus open or

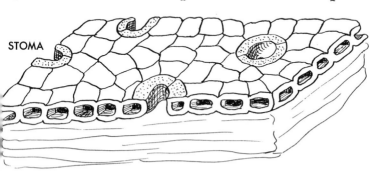

PROTECTIVE LAYER OF CELLS FROM UNDERSIDE
OF A LEAF, SHOWING STOMATA

close the little "mouths." These cells are called guard cells and it is a good name for them. They guard the plant so it does not lose too much water, and yet they allow enough water through by opening up to keep the system of soil-water conduction in efficient operation.

Light is partly responsible for the action of the guard cells. The stomata of the older leaves open in the daytime and close at night. Young leaves may not open their stomata at all during the day. They need all the water they can get in order to grow.

The amount of water vapor in the air affects the guard cells too. Frequently just before rain begins to fall the air contains a great deal of water vapor. Ordinarily open stomata will release gaseous water. However, because the air is already saturated, they cannot do so. So the stem twists, turning the leaf over and exposing the stomata to the air above, where air currents can move more freely and thus permit greater operation. Some people believe this is why many of the leaves of a tree turn over when rain is in the offing.

The effect of light on stomata is not direct. Light helps to form a special chemical substance in the guard cells. This substance changes starch to sugar inside the cell. The sugar causes the guard cells to become turgid, or reach their full size, thus enlarging the opening.

An experiment with the effect of light on stomata will show this to be true. Any one of the following plants may be used in your experiment. Two varieties that have large stomata are wandering Jew, a common house plant, and common plantain, a well-known lawn and garden weed. Boston fern works well also. You will probably remember having seen all three of these plants.

BOSTON FERN

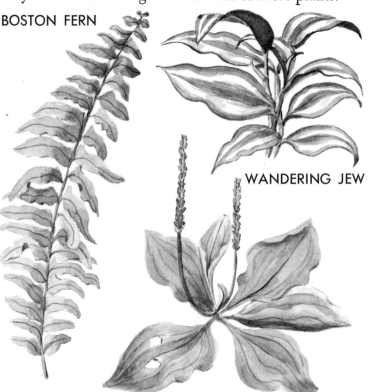

WANDERING JEW

COMMON PLANTAIN

Select a leaf and roll it between your fingers to loosen the outer layers. With a razor blade scrape two pieces of skin, or epidermis, from the underside of the leaf you choose to work with. Place the pieces on separate slides, cover with water, and drop cover slips on them. Place under low power and look for stomata, which will look like open eyes. Your first pieces may not have stomata, but keep mounting—you will eventually find some. When you have two mounts containing stomata, place one in a completely dark, damp place (in a saucer of water placed in a dark closet) and keep the other moist and exposed to light.

The guard cells in the light will appear turgid because they contain sugar; they will be expanded to full size and therefore the opening or stoma between the guard cells will be expanded. This is somewhat like the effect produced when an inner tube is filled with air. After the other stoma has been in the dark for about half an hour, place it under the low power. It will be apparent that these guard cells are less turgid than those in the other preparation and that the opening between the guard cells has therefore diminished in size.

Before you leave this fascinating system of pipes, strip off one string from a stalk of celery and examine it under low power to see how the water pipes are made. Notice

how the walls are constructed of a special kind of cell
just right for this kind of job. They look like little rec-
tangles. The inside of the water-conducting pipe looks as
though it were lined with tiles.

Be sure you keep a record on cards of what you have
found as suggested in chapter 7, and indicate especially
what problems you encountered and how you solved
them.

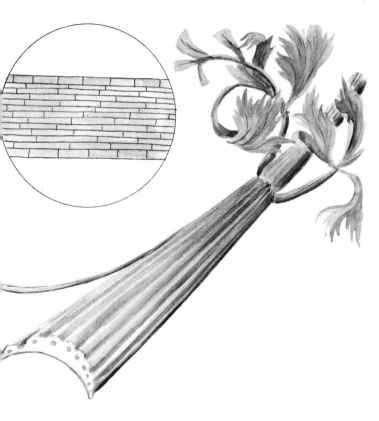

CHAPTER SEVEN

Keeping Records
of Your Research

YOU HAVE had a lot of fun looking at many different things, and you have learned how to make permanent mounts of your specimens. Now let us take time out to explore why we are making these observations, why we are mounting our specimens, and what we are going to do about our findings and observations.

Men of science—men like Louis Pasteur, Robert Koch, Jonas Salk, Walter Reed, Alexander Fleming—are all, or were, keen observers. They have trained themselves to use their eyes to find out everything possible from the things around them. They are so busy looking and they see so many things in their laboratories that they dare not trust themselves to memorize the details of their observations. So they record their findings. Everything they have seen, every event that has occurred on the stage of their microscopes, is entered in their notebooks. It is from such evidence, accumulated over the years, that men draw conclusions that often point the way research must go in order to make vital discoveries—new findings concerned with the cause, cure, and prevention of disease; the preservation of food; the structure of metals.

Your observations and your findings will have little meaning to you until you train yourself to observe carefully. You must see only those things that are actually in the field of your microscope. You must keep from believing you see things when they do not actually exist. The value of your observations will be increased many times if you keep records of the things you do and the events that take place.

A card catalog is an efficient device for keeping records. Small cards (3 by 5 inches) are easy to handle and to sort. They can be stored easily. New methods of organizing can be started at any time—something that is difficult to do if records are kept on large sheets or in a notebook. The cards themselves are durable.

Part of the fun of research and investigation is devising your own system of records. However, you may need a few suggestions in order to get started. Here is a sample card. Note that the entries are brief, yet the card contains a great deal of information. A year or more from the

```
┌─────────────────────────────────────────────────┐
│                                                   │
│  SLIDE No. 85         DATE: July 18, 19··         │
│                       Enlargement: 50 x           │
│                                                   │
│  Specimen:  Fly's wing.                           │
│  Where found:  In my Kitchen at Velma,            │
│                                  Ohio.            │
│                                                   │
│  Appearance: Filmy, lacy, many colored            │
│  (iridescent), delicate, fuzzy at joint.          │
│  Remarks: Mounted in Duco cement.                 │
│  Compare with slide 86, other wing of fly,        │
│  mounted in balsam.                               │
│                                                   │
└─────────────────────────────────────────────────┘
```

time you start your file you could turn to this card and your researches could be repeated in the same manner, or you could find the results if such a procedure were to be followed again. Also, you can measure your own growth. Five or six years from now you can turn back to your file and find useful the things you did when you were a high school student. You may find some errors too. A good scientist learns a great deal from his own mistakes.

The sample card shown here would be better if a drawing of the wing were on the reverse side. There are several ways of making a drawing. One way is to look carefully at the wing through the microscope and then draw from memory, switching back and forth until the drawing is complete. This is better than making no drawing at all; but it is not a good method, for errors can creep in.

A better way, one that makes for a more accurate representation, is to train yourself to see the image through the microscope with one eye and the drawing with the other eye. The operation sounds quite impossible, but it can be done after a little practice—in much the same manner that you trained yourself to look through the microscope with both eyes open. When you draw in this manner the image in your brain is of the pencil point moving along the actual specimen. You can thus make an accurate drawing.

It is essential that you file your slides with care. Here again the organization should be according to your own special interests. Often it is desirable to place together all those slides concerned with a single insect—a fly, for instance. Or it may be preferable to file together those mounts of certain insect parts—wings or legs or mouth parts. Number the slides and keep a notebook of the numbers and the specimens they contain.

Wooden boxes designed for storing slides are inexpensive and we suggest that you buy a few of these. However, temporary storage boxes can be made in the following manner. Make two folds, each 1 inch from the edge,

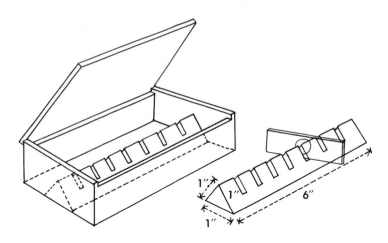

along the long axis of a piece of cardboard 3 by 6 inches. Fasten the edges together so you have a triangular cross section that is 1 inch on each side. Glue this to the bottom of a cigar box. Make cuts with a razor blade ½ inch deep in the triangle and then place your slides in these cuts. Be sure the cuts are wide enough so the cover slips do not rub against the edges.

Another quick way to build a slide box is shown here. Cut out a piece of heavy cardboard in the shape shown. The bottom of the box should be just wide enough to accommodate a slide. Lay a slide on the cardboard to get the proper dimension. The sides of the box are as high as a slide is wide. Line the sides of the box with corrugated paper from a cardboard carton or candy box. This will serve as guides for the slides. Fasten the whole box together with Scotch Tape. A cover can be made by laying out a second cardboard and increasing the dimensions by a little bit in each direction.

Organize your work to suit your own interests. The important thing is that the work is not slipshod and haphazard, but that it is thorough, neat, and well put together.

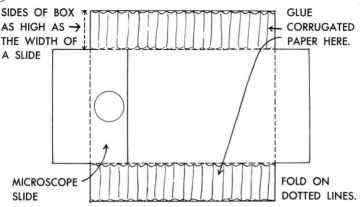

SIDES OF BOX ↗
AS HIGH AS →
THE WIDTH OF
A SLIDE

GLUE
← CORRUGATED
PAPER HERE.

MICROSCOPE
SLIDE

FOLD ON
DOTTED LINES.

PLAN OF SLIDE BOX

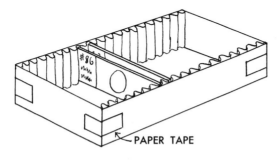

PAPER TAPE

COMPLETED SLIDE BOX

CHAPTER EIGHT

Culturing Protozoa

AFTER YOU have learned to handle the microscope with ease and have looked at a lot of things that stay quiet under the cover slip, you are ready to examine something that moves. In many books about living things you will find pictures of what can be seen in a drop of water, similar to the illustration at the end of the chapter.

But this water is not tap water. Tap water does not contain living organisms large enough to see under the microscope. It may contain bacteria but they are extremely tiny. Furthermore, there are never many of them in drinking water. You would need a special lens on your microscope and other special equipment for encouraging the bacteria to grow before you could see them. The drop of water shown in many biology books is a drop of pond water and it is one that has been specially handled. The rain water standing in small puddles on grassy fields or in ditches frequently contains many little animals called protozoa. About ten thousand different varieties of these tiny one-celled organisms are known. You might wonder how they get into the puddle. Are they made from the soil directly? Do they fall in the rain? Are they in the soil all the time and merely wait for a rain so that they can all go swimming? Actually the latter thought is the nearest to the truth. They come from the stems of the grasses and they go swimming in the rain water. But they also multiply quickly when conditions are right.

They need water for a full active life. But if their puddle dries up—and rain puddles do eventually—they adapt themselves to the conditions. They grow a sort of case or shell called a cyst around their single-celled bodies and barely hold onto life until rain falls and lets them swim free again. In this respect they are somewhat like seeds, which show no signs of life until they are given the proper conditions of soil, warmth, and water.

The surfaces of twigs, grass, and leaves in dried-up ponds and ditches usually contain thousands of these microorganisms, each snug in its case and much too tiny to see even with a magnifying glass. These encased protozoa can be made active again by placing them in what is called a hay infusion. An infusion is a specially prepared liquid in which it is possible to make organisms

65

MODEL OF STENTOR

MODEL OF SIMPLE RING COLONY
(Cyclonexus annularis)

grow. This is called culturing the protozoa, and the collection of microorganisms you make in this way is called a culture.

Find a place along a field or roadway or a park or vacant lot where water usually stands for quite some time following a rainstorm. Be sure the place is free of oil or other materials that might interfere with living things. Collect some of the grass and twigs from this spot. Include a few grass plants with the roots attached.

Get two clean large-mouthed jars with loose covers. Hold some of the grasses and twigs over a jar and cut them into pieces ½ to ¾ inch long, allowing the grass to fall into the jar freely as it is cut. Fill the jar one-quarter full, no more. Prepare the second jar in the same way.

Catch some rain water in a nonmetallic container. It will remain clear and suitable for your experiments until molds develop in it. This will take two weeks or so. Pour in rain water to fill each jar within one inch of the top. If you cannot collect rain water, use distilled water obtainable from a drugstore. Tap water frequently contains chlorine which has been put in to kill bacteria that might have found their way into the water. It will hardly do for a swimming pool for our little fellows. However, if you allow tap water to stand for two or three days and pour it back and forth from one container to another a few times, most of the chlorine will pass off into the air and the tap water may then be used.

Place the tops on the jars loosely and put one infusion in a warm—but not hot—place. It should be kept in the light, but not in bright sunlight. Put the second jar in a warm, *dark* place. After two or three days you are ready to go hunting. Using a medicine dropper, draw up some of the liquid from near the top of the infusion that was kept in the light. Take the liquid from a place near a piece of grass or a twig. Hold the dropper in a vertical position for a few seconds over a microscope slide. This allows the heavier material, which includes some of the protozoa, you hope, to fall to the bottom of the dropper. Place just *one* drop on the slide.

Shred up a few bits of lens paper or tease out a few fibers from a small tuft of cotton. These fibers are to be used to trap the little beasts. Drop these fibers into the water on the slide. Cover the drop with a clean cover slip. The drop should be just large enough to spread out and cover the whole area under the cover slip. If there is too much liquid, it will ooze out from under the thin glass slip, making it messy to handle. The excess water may be picked up with a corner of a blotter. A little practice will show you how big a drop to take.

Place the slide under the microscope, arrange the light,

and focus the instrument. If you are lucky, you will find the field filled with moving animals. Sometimes they slither by at a fast pace. Some of them stay more or less in the same place and only turn round and round like a micro-dog chasing its tail. Some open and shut like a flower with huge petals.

The cotton or lens-paper fibers can be seen sprawling across the field. Within the spaces between individual fibers you may occasionally find a sort of corral in which one or more protozoa are trapped and cannot escape. This gives you an opportunity to examine them in a more leisurely fashion. Some of the types do not move at all but remain anchored to bits of debris in the drop. Hunt carefully along a section of the grayish, cloudy stuff that frequently is found in the drop. Some of the protozoa may be found attached to some of this material by a sort of foot. They may reach out and draw back at intervals.

If you want to slow up the microorganisms so you can see them better, you can place a drop of rubbing alcohol near the edge of the cover slip. This will work in under the slip and, when it strikes the protozoa, it slows them. It eventually kills them, of course.

Try several drops from the top of the culture and then move your hunting ground farther down in the jar. Try both places in the jar that has been kept in the dark.

Some kinds of protozoa grow faster if the culturing is done in the dark. Note which jar produces protozoa first and look for differences in the kinds of microorganisms produced in each jar.

Record the kinds of animals you see by making a sketch of each species. Indicate also the kinds which seem most abundant. Note at what depth in the culture each type appears. The increase in numbers can then be noted each day for a couple of weeks. The culture usually reaches its peak in about a week or ten days. All during this time new kinds show up every day or so. The members of the first observed species may die out or may continue. You may be able to find one variety that attacks another and get in on a fight to the death beneath the surface of a drop of pond water.

Many of these protozoa reproduce by splitting in two and forming two new perfect organisms. If you have the patience to watch a single one long enough, you will be able to follow through this fascinating operation. It is called binary fission, which is only a fancy way of saying "splitting in two."

Although some of the larger protozoa are big enough to be seen with the naked eye or with a hand magnifying glass, it takes technique and practice to catch a single organism. If you can catch a single cell in a fine medicine dropper, you can raise a whole culture of all one kind of protozoans with this as a starter. This is then called a pure culture.

First you will need to prepare a solution in which the single microorganism can be placed to grow. Make a soup by boiling some dry grass in water for 20 minutes. Include some grass plant heads containing seeds if possible. Let the soup stand until the heavy particles settle, then pour off the clear liquid into several glass jars. Baby-food jars are excellent. The boiling will kill all cysts of microorganism and most of the bacteria. Allow the jars to remain open until the soup begins to grow bacteria. You can tell when this growth begins by observing a thin, grayish scum on the top. These bacteria will serve as food for the larger microorganisms you plan to raise. A soup like this is called a culture medium. There are scores of kinds of culture media. Each kind must contain exactly the materials necessary for the greatest growth of the particular organism the scientist is trying to produce in quantity.

Most medicine droppers have too large an opening for effectively snaring a single protozoan. The solution to this problem is to make some capillary tubes or pipettes. Your science teacher will be glad to make some for you. A piece of soft glass tubing is first softened by rotating it

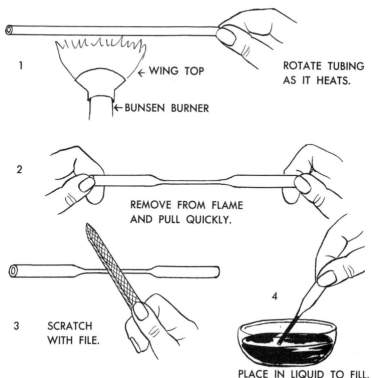

1 ← WING TOP

ROTATE TUBING AS IT HEATS.

← BUNSEN BURNER

2 REMOVE FROM FLAME AND PULL QUICKLY.

3 SCRATCH WITH FILE.

4

PLACE IN LIQUID TO FILL.

MAKING A CAPILLARY PIPETTE

over a wing-top burner. The tubing is then removed and pulled quickly from both ends. A tube similar to the one in the illustration results. Scratch the thin part of the tube with a file and break it from the ends. The hole in the capillary tube is so tiny that liquid will run right up it, the way oil runs up a lamp wick. The word "capillary" comes from the Latin word *capillus* which means "hair."

The opening in these pipettes is frequently no bigger around than a hair.

Place a drop of water from your hay infusion on a slide. Examine it under lower power to be sure that you have a good collection of protozoa. Place the tip of the capillary tube in the drop and let some of the liquid rise up in the thin tube. Now transfer some *small* droplets from the capillary tube to fresh slides. You can form small drops by blowing gently into the large end of the tube. Examine each small drop until you find one that holds a single protozoan. Clean the capillary tube before each immersion by dipping it in very hot water and then in very cold water. You will speed up your work, of course, if you have several capillary tubes and use a fresh one each time. You can then clean the whole collection at once.

Touch a clean pipette to the small droplet and draw up the protozoan. Examine the capillary with a hand glass or under low power to be sure that you have trapped your victim. Blow out the contents of the pipette gently into one of the waiting jars of prepared culture medium.

Transfer as many organisms in this way as you have jars but keep one jar of culture media free of protozoans as a control. Cover each jar loosely with a saucer and put

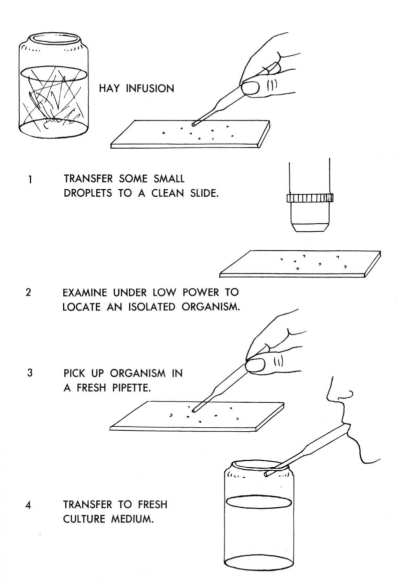

HAY INFUSION

1 TRANSFER SOME SMALL
DROPLETS TO A CLEAN SLIDE.

2 EXAMINE UNDER LOW POWER TO
LOCATE AN ISOLATED ORGANISM.

3 PICK UP ORGANISM IN
A FRESH PIPETTE.

4 TRANSFER TO FRESH
CULTURE MEDIUM.

CATCHING A SINGLE PROTOZOAN

FREE-LIVING PROTOZOA

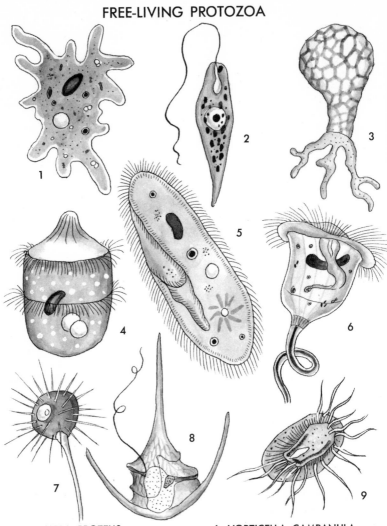

1. AMEBA PROTEUS
2. EUGLENA VIRIDIS
3. DIFFLUGIA OBLONGA
4. DIDINIUM NASUTUM
5. PARAMECIUM CAUDATUM
6. VORTICELLA CAMPANULA
7. EPHELOTA CORONATA
8. CERATIUM SP.
9. EUPLOTES PATELLA

them in a warm place. Within a day or two the growth of many microorganisms from the single one will become apparent. By the end of a week you may be able to see the cloud of protozoans with your naked eye. The control jar should remain free of protozoans but it may become cloudy from the number of bacteria that have grown where no organisms were around to eat them up. Some jars may produce no protozoans at all because your "seed" organism was injured during the transfer. That is why it is a good idea to start several jars.

The fact that so many organisms have grown into a pure culture starting from just one is good proof that in the beginning stages of growth, at least, the protozoans must have reproduced by binary fission. Pure cultures of this kind may be kept alive by transferring some of the old culture to new media every week. Science teachers are frequently interested in obtaining pure cultures for class work, and you may start a small business supplying protozoans.

Some of the types of protozoa you are most likely to find are shown in the illustration here. Don't let the long names scare you. After you have worked with some of these little beasties for a while, you will use their names as easily as you learned to say Schenectady and Milwaukee and Indianapolis.

CHAPTER NINE

Textiles

THE CLOTHES on your back provide rich fields to be explored with your microscope. You can discover that the fibers from which threads are made have characteristics which give them distinctive properties and that fabrics vary a great deal in the way the threads are put together.

First let's look at cotton. A piece from an old sheet or shirt will do. Loosen a strand or two with the point of a needle. Fray this strand so the individual fibers are separated and then place the frayed strand in a drop of water on a slide. Cover it with a cover glass.

When you look at the cotton fibers with a magnification of 100 diameters they appear nearly smooth and regular. Under higher powers, the fibers appear flat and twisted. Better grades of cotton are made of long, even fibers which make the finished fabric smooth and long wearing. Try various cottons to see similarities and differences. Make several slides until you have one in which the fibers show up clearly. Mount in balsam the fibers you intend to keep for further study and comparison. Number them and file them in your slide box. Record the number in your notebook and enter the source from which it was obtained.

Now get a small piece of pure woolen yarn. Yarn is likely to be unused or virgin wool. Separate a single strand with a needle point and then fray the strand to obtain a single fiber. Here again the fiber may appear smooth under low magnification; however, when the power is increased, the fibers are seen to be made of a series of scales that overlap each other. In virgin wool the scales are more pronounced. They look somewhat like the scales on a fish or snake. If you do not see the scales at first, vary the light coming through the stage. You may get better results by cutting out the substage light completely and lighting from the side with a flashlight or desk lamp held above the stage. Prepare a permanent mount that shows the typical structure of this type of fiber as illustrated on page 81. Wool is hair from a sheep. Compare it with a human hair.

Linen fibers prepared in the same manner will appear to be segmented. The fiber comes from a flax plant which has long slender cells joined end to end. In the flax plant these fibers conduct liquids through the stem and give the stem its strength. They are somewhat like the strings in celery in this regard. The fibers are removed by soaking the stems and rotting away the rest of the material. The structure of linen fibers makes them strong and long lasting.

Silk is another natural fiber that is interesting under the microscope. Actually it is spun by a silkworm to make a covering for its cocoon. Each fiber is one long, shiny filament. The evenness of the fibers produces a fine, smooth fabric—the silken touch.

In your work with textiles you will come across synthetics, either pure or combined with wool, cotton, or silk. Make slides of nylon, rayon, Orlon, Dacron, and any other man-made fiber you can obtain. You will discover that such fibers are invariably smooth and regular, similar to silk. In fact, they are like silk because they are made in much the same manner that a worm makes silk. They are formed by forcing a solution through tiny holes in a device called a spinneret. The liquid solidifies after it passes out of the holes in the spinneret and into a hardening acid bath.

Now you have four slides representing the four natural fibers—cotton, wool, linen, and silk. These were obtained

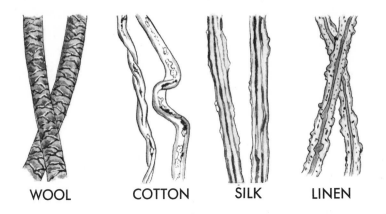

WOOL   COTTON   SILK   LINEN

from known fabrics. You can use them to compare with unknown fibers as a basis of identification. You also have labeled slides of some of the synthetic fibers which may serve you in the same manner, although identification of synthetics by means of a microscope is almost impossible for amateurs.

Let us put the slides to work. Ask your mother to give you a piece of material. Ask her to remember the composition of the material (50 per cent cotton and 50 per cent nylon, let us say). It is your job to study the fibers out of which the fabric is made and tell her the composition. Compare the fibers in the unknown material with those on your sample slides. If your master slides are made carefully, you should be able to identify the fibers without fail: linen, cotton, or wool. Smooth fibers will usually be one of the synthetics, which cannot be identified more definitely by a microscope. Maybe it's silk and maybe it isn't. Only a chemist can tell the difference.

A further guide to the identification of fibers is the cross-sectional view. You can make cross-section slides of fibers by embedding some threads in paraffin and cutting sections with a homemade microtome as described in chapter 4. Experiment to find which thickness is most appropriate for your purposes. When you have a section that shows clearly the detail of the fiber you want to study, mount this permanently and file it with your textile slides.

Your father can get you a good cross section of human hair if he will shave close a second time and rinse out his razor in clear water. He will not mind being a human microtome if he thinks that it will aid your study! Hairs taken from furs or from the coats of animals make an interesting collection. Police laboratories frequently have a collection of slides of hairs of all kinds, flat, round, wispy, depending on the animal from which it comes. Bits of hair found at the scene of a crime are sometimes important evidence. They may be human hairs or the hair of the family cat, and it is essential that the police be sure which kind it is.

Science instructors frequently use two different colored fibers crossed and mounted on the same slide. The student is asked to tell which fiber is on top. It is a good way to find out if the student knows how to focus a microscope properly.

The identifying of the fibers in materials is an absorbing interest. Also there are many other things you can do to broaden your knowledge of fabrics. For example, you can discover the various ways in which threads are joined together in fabrics—each method offering certain advantages. Cloth is made by stretching a lot of threads parallel to each other to begin with. These threads are called the warp. Other threads, the weft, or woof, are woven in and out among the warp threads by the loom. The conventional method of joining fibers is by weaving each weft thread over and under adjacent warp threads. Look at a handkerchief under low power and you will see this pattern.

Occasionally this standard weave is modified by having the weft threads go over one warp thread and under

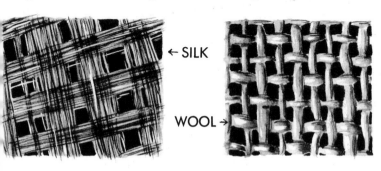

← SILK

WOOL →

two, over one and under two, and so on. Or the weft threads may go over one warp thread and under three, four, five, or up to as many as ten. The resulting fabrics will have many variations. If the weft threads are thin and the warp are thick, the fabric is different in texture. Such materials are called twills. The sort of weave called bird's-eye arranges fibers in small eyelike figures interesting to see under the microscope. Bird's-eye cloth was among your first experiences. It is used commonly in diapers!

Hosiery and other clothing is made by knitting fibers rather than weaving them. Caps, hats, and blazers are often made by felting fibers. "Felting" means pushing fibers together every which way and cementing them so they hold permanently. Frequently fibers are neither woven nor knit but are worked into complicated patterns in nets and laces.

Make slides of different materials to show composition and texture. Try to get a number of different styles of weave. Remember to label your slides and to enter information in your notebook or on 3-by-5 cards so that you have a permanent record of your progress. Textiles are an interesting study and one about which there is much to be learned. These early studies of yours may lead to an interesting career in this important field.

CHAPTER TEN

Molds

MOLDS ARE interesting little plants and they are common enough to provide a good source of specimens for the student of microscopy. They grow rapidly, too. Large mold growths can begin from a single spore. The spores of mold are very tiny cases which are found floating about in the air nearly everywhere. The dust lying on the table top will generally have a number of spores of bread mold in it. These spores can withstand great extremes of temperature and can remain dry for years without losing their ability to grow. They only need moisture and a warm, dark place to bring them to life. There are molds which will grow on fruit, on old shoes, on bookbindings, floor boards, and wood paneling if conditions are right. They are unable to manufacture food for themselves so they must grow on a material that will supply them with the nutrients they need.

Moisten several pieces of bread by sprinkling water from your fingers and wipe them across a table top. Put them away in separate Mason jars or other closed containers in a warm, dark place. After a day or two examine them. On at least one you will probably find a fluffy white growth that looks like cotton. Tiny black dots will be peppered all over it. This plant is the common bread mold. Mount some of the material in a drop of water mixed with a drop of alcohol. See page 41. Some of the pieces of bread may have black, green, or pink mold growths which have forced out the bread mold and obtained a firm footing for themselves. We'll come to these later in this chapter.

Under the microscope you will find a collection of filaments. Follow one of these along by moving the slide and changing the focus until you come to a place where several other filaments branch out. At the end of one of these side branches you will find a round case filled with spores. This case is called a sporangium. If the culture is at the proper period of its growth, you may find that some of these sporangia have burst and are liberating literally thousands of spores. The microscope will give you some idea of how infinitely tiny the spores are. You can see why there are always enough of them to go around and why they float so freely in air.

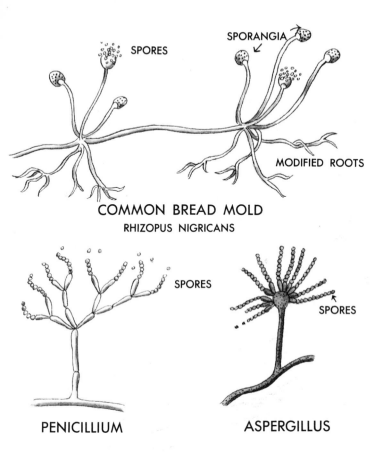

SPORES

SPORANGIA

MODIFIED ROOTS

COMMON BREAD MOLD
RHIZOPUS NIGRICANS

SPORES

SPORES

PENICILLIUM   ASPERGILLUS

From the first joining place on the filament, from which the sporangia branches, you will find a system of branching threads that look like a root system (see illustration). These serve as anchors for the mold plants. Through these anchors the plants suck up the food materials they need to keep going.

Other filaments shoot out from a junction place. They work like the runners of a strawberry plant. A single mold plant, once established, can send out one or more of these runners and start a new plant. This plant in turn can send out another runner. If the food held out and other conditions were proper, the mold could eventually cover everything in the world.

The common bread mold is called *Rhizopus nigricans*. *Rhizopus* means "root-footed." It has "walking" roots. *Nigricans* is used to indicate the black appearance of its sporangia. Molds have none of the green coloring (chlorophyll, an ingredient necessary for food-making) which is common to higher plants. This is the reason that they cannot manufacture their own food but must rob it from sources already prepared.

If some of your bread pieces produce an all-black mold, don't miss seeing it. It is sometimes called black mildew. Its scientific name is *Aspergillus*. Your mother has grown some when she didn't intend to if she ever stored clothes when they were damp or left the ironing too long after sprinkling. Be sure to dry your tent out thoroughly before you store it for the winter or you will find how destructive this black mildew can be on cloth.

Aspergillus produces thousands of spores. Search through a prepared mount of the black mildew to see if you can find any spores just beginning to germinate or sprout. If you catch the *Aspergillus* before it is too old, you will find a lot of brushlike growths at the end of some of the filaments. These brushes are made up of chains of spore cases at the tip of a branch. The mold is named for these little brushes. In some churches a small brush is used to sprinkle holy water. It is called an aspergillum which means, literally, a little sprinkler. Housewives sometimes sprinkle water on clothes from a wet whisk broom which looks somewhat like *Aspergillus* brushes.

The bluish-green mold you will find growing on your bread medium is the most interesting of all. It is a species of *Penicillium*. One strain of a particular species of this mold was found growing on a decaying melon. It was found to be a strain which produced a superior type of penicillin. It is grown in large quantities and the penicillin is extracted from the growing mold. Home-canned fruits and jellies frequently have bits of this mold growing on them. The spores get in through caps which are not tight enough or fall into the jelly while it is cooling and is still exposed to the air of the kitchen. The mold is extremely common on oranges. If you find some of this blue-green *Penicillium* on your bread samples, you can transfer it to a good orange and get a growth which shows all the stages of development of the mold.

Under the microscope you will find a brush structure on *Penicillium* too. *Penicillium* is named from the Latin *penicillus*—a paint brush. The first writing was done with a brush and our modern writing tool—the pencil—gets its name from these old-fashioned brushes.

Streak a knife blade several times through the blue-green mold. Use this knife to cut deep into the skin of a good orange in a few places. Put the orange into a jar with a cover. Put some wet cotton at the bottom of the jar to keep the interior moist. Keep the jar in a warm and dark place for a week or ten days. Examine some of the new blue-green mold. A large growth sometimes has tiny amber drops on it. These drops contain the material from which penicillin is extracted. In industry the mold is grown in huge tanks on specially prepared nutrient liquids.

A different mold growth can be made from dead flies. Place several dead flies in a covered jar containing a small wet sponge. Keep in a warm place. In four or five days the flies will be covered with a cottony growth. This white stuff is made of mold filaments. Mount some of this in water and look for egg-shaped or oval swimming spores. The swimming spores are formed in the tip ends of the filaments. Some filament tips will appear cloudy; some will be filled with what look like tiny marbles.

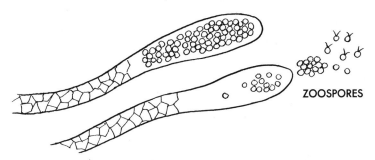

ZOOSPORES

ENDS OF FILAMENTS OF SAPROLEGNIA,
SHOWING SWIMMING SPORES

From some tips you may find the spores swarming out. These spores are equipped with little threadlike tails which they use to propel themselves through the water. They are called zoospores because they move more like animals than plants.

Since this mold lives in water all the time it must form new colonies by moving through the water to its new pasture land. A mold that causes one form of potato rot produces zoospores which can move through soil in the same way. The mold lives on dead and decaying things and is called *Saprolegnia.* The root word *sapro* means "putrid" or "rotten." The spores are attracted to decaying things and actually swim toward them to establish a new outbreak of mold. Air-borne molds must depend on chance winds to bring them to the proper kind of food material. Live fish in an aquarium are sometimes infected

91

with one of these water-borne molds. The molds spread so rapidly that they can kill a fish that becomes attacked.

Molds are fungi. Bacteria and yeasts are fungi, too. There are about 100,000 species of fungi so, if you become interested in this phase of microscope work, don't worry about running out of specimens! Each one of these fungi has a name. Each of the kinds, like the molds, has names too for special parts. How does anyone go about learning all these names? No one remembers them all, of course, but the trick we have used in this chapter of tying up the name of the organism or its part with something about the organism is a great help. It helps if you have actually observed the plant or animal first. It is valuable then to write a note about it. This aids in fixing the term in your mind. A good background of Latin and Greek root words is of assistance too. The names of many organisms are so interesting that, rather than being drudgery, the learning of the proper term to apply to microscopic objects is a fascinating game in itself.

CHAPTER ELEVEN

Yeasts and Other One-Celled Forms

ANOTHER GROUP of plants with no chlorophyll, under the general class of fungi, are the yeasts. To most of us yeast implies the little square cake wrapped in foil that we get at the grocery store. This is only one variety of yeast. Actually there are hundreds of species. The yeasts' main claim to fame is their ability to break down sugar into alcohol and carbon dioxide gas. Sometimes we are after the first of these products, as in the brewing industry. At other times, as in baking bread, it is the gas produced by the growing yeasts that puffs up the dough and makes a more palatable loaf. Yeast has been used for the latter job for centuries. One of the tombs at Thebes contained loaves of bread which had been left as an offering for the dead. Yeast cells were identified in this bread and in that from other tombs. The date of the Theban tomb was 2000 B.C.

93

Yeasts get their food for growth from sugar. They apparently attack the sugar by giving out a substance called an enzyme, or a ferment. The process is called fermentation. You have undoubtedly seen some food stuffs that are "working," or fermenting. The characteristic odor of fermentation is partly due to the alcohol. The alcohol produced in breadmaking leaves the loaf in the oven.

Let us take a look at these little single-celled plants. So-called wild yeasts, like molds, are found in the air all the time. Apple juice allowed to stand open in a warm room will soon show signs of fermentation. Yeasts in the air have dropped into it and have begun their work. Fresh sauerkraut—not the canned kind—will have many yeasts still alive in it. They are partly responsible for changing the cabbage to kraut. The scum on dill pickles is made up mainly of yeast cells.

If you have none of these sources of yeast cultures, you can grow a culture quickly from a crumbled bit of commercial yeast cake. Yeast cakes consist of yeast cells mixed with starch. Add the bit of cake to a solution made of a spoonful of sugar in a tumblerful of lukewarm water. Be sure that the water is not too hot. This can kill the yeasts. Corn syrup works even better than table sugar. Stir the solution so you have an even, milky suspension. Let the yeast grow overnight in this solution.

The room must be warm. Too low a temperature slows down the growth of yeasts or prevents it entirely. If you keep this solution for a few days you can detect the odor of alcohol in it.

To observe the yeasts, place a drop of the milky liquid on a slide. Prepare a dilute iodine solution by adding 1 drop of tincture of iodine to about 20 drops of water. Put a drop of this solution on the slide with the yeast preparation. The iodine serves two purposes. It darkens the nuclei of the yeast cells and stains the starch grains. The yeast cells are almost transparent and are a little difficult to see. You can recognize the starch grains easily because the iodine reacts with them to produce a blue color. Cut the light down as far as possible with the adjustment under the stage of the microscope, if your instrument is so equipped. If you have no such adjustment, move the mirror to reduce the illumination.

Look for yeast cells in several stages of growth. In the first stage the cell has a large, clear space in it called a vacuole. There is a tiny nucleus in this vacuole. In the second stage the vacuole has disappeared and a large nucleus can be seen. This nucleus begins to form a waist and looks like an hourglass in the third stage. The cell itself has, by this time, begun to draw out into a similar shape and the cell is said to be forming a bud. This bud

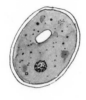

YEAST CELL
SHOWING VACUOLE

NUCLEUS
FORMED

BUDDING
BEGINNING

DIVISION COMPLETE;
"MOTHER" AND
"DAUGHTER" CELL
SEPARATE.

YEAST CELL HIGHLY MAGNIFIED

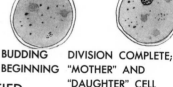

A CHAIN OF YEAST SPORES

finally pulls away from the mother cell entirely and is a new and complete yeast cell ready to go through the same four stages itself.

A cell may have more than one bud. Sometimes the cells stick together for a time and remain in long, irregular chains. Eventually all the new cells break loose and continue to form buds and new cells of their own. Almost all single-celled organisms reproduce by cell division of one sort or another. Budding is one type of cell division. As long as there is food present, yeasts will continue to multiply.

In addition to fungi, another large division of plants is the algae. A member of this division is a simple single-celled plant called *Protococcus*. This organism is responsible for the green growth on the shady side of trees and rocks in moist environments. It can be found in growing condition at any time of year. Bring home some small pieces of bark showing a decided green growth. Soak the bark in water for an hour or so. Carefully scrape off a little of the green material and transfer it to a drop of water on a slide. The *Protococcus* cells are spheres or ovals when they are free to float in the water.

The green growth is frequently made up of other organisms that grow along with the *Protococcus.* But look carefully through the collection of cells on the slide until you find a *Protococcus* cell pinched in the middle. This is a cell about to split into two cells. This process is binary fission, which you met under protozoa. As you will see, this way of producing new cells is different from that used by the yeasts. In the culture you may find large groups of cells stuck together. Sometimes the two daughter cells formed by the binary fission continue to stick together for a time and each continues to split into two new cells. Eventually the cells break away from

 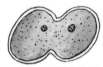 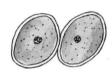

SINGLE CELL   FISSION BEGINNING   FISSION COMPLETE
BINARY FISSION IN PROTOCOCCUS

these masses and, if the colony should dry out, these cells are blown about by the wind until they find a suitable location for beginning life all over again.

Pollen grains from flowers are wind borne too. They look much like spores under the microscope. Many pollen grains, however, have intricate designs on their outer walls. It is possible to distinguish the pollen of one flower from that of another. This is important to beekeepers, who want to know what flowers their little workers are visiting. It is useful, too, to people studying the kinds of plants that cause the so-called hay-fever allergy. Most hay fever is really due to plants other than the grasses.

Pollen grains are not single-celled plants, although they may look like them. They are only part of a plant. They must land on a flower and grow a long filament which moves down a tube in the second flower, reaches the egg, and fertilizes it. Apparently there is a material secreted by the second plant that starts the growth of the pollen grain when it lands in the proper place on the flower to carry out its fertilization chore.

GOATSBEARD   TULIP TREE   ROSE   POLLEN GRAIN GERMINATING

RAGWEED POLLEN
photographed with electron microscope

Pollen grains will grow on the sugar solution you have prepared. We might as well discuss them here while you have all the culture material ready. Place a drop of sugar water on a slide. Sprinkle the pollen from a flower into the solution by tapping a newly opened flower over the slide. Lilies are particularly rich in pollen. Petunias give up their pollen readily. Any flower you find with a powdery dust in such a position in the blossom that it can easily be shaken out will do. After you have shaken out the pollen, put a small bowl over the slide and let it stand for 1 hour.

Search the slide for pollen grains that have begun to sprout. A part of their cell wall will grow out to form a long filament. Many times you can actually watch this filament get longer under the microscope. The tube turns this way and that as it grows. In this way the tube would find the proper place to enter so that fertilization of the flower might be completed. The sugar solution serves the same purpose as the material present on the flower where the pollen must grow to fulfill its function.

As you look back over the experiences of this chapter you can't help but notice how a little knowledge of what to look for increases your enjoyment at the microscope. To the untrained eye, yeasts, *Protococcus,* and pollen grains look merely like little circles or balls under the microscope. If you know what to look for, however, each of these tiny spheres has a different story to tell you.

But do not stop your investigations here, for there are many other sources rich in materials to study.

Get as many different flowers as you can. Collect pollen from these flowers and study it under your microscope to see the great variation there is among the grains, even though they all serve the same function—fertilization of the cells that will become seeds.

Protococcus is only one of hundreds of algae. Hunt for other specimens in the woods, in brooks and springs, ponds and lakes. Each plant you find will have characteristics that will challenge your ability to investigate.

Your microscope can open a multitude of avenues for research. All that is required is your ambition and desire to follow them. Keep records as you progress, so you will always be able to recall the discoveries you have made, as well as the direction in which you are moving.

CHAPTER TWELVE

Blood

ONE OF the greatest thrills at the microscope for many people comes when they first see their own blood on a slide. Blood is one of those materials that is usually forgotten until we cut ourselves. Most people know in a vague way that blood circulates around the body. They may know that an adult man has about five quarts of blood. This is the same volume as the oil in the crankcase of your father's automobile. You probably know, too, that blood contains corpuscles. But have you ever seen them? And have you ever seen blood circulate through the vessels of an animal?

Blood is really a marvelous fluid. It carries foodstuffs and removes wastes. It tears down the banks of the rivers of the body through which it flows and then builds up the banks again as it goes by.

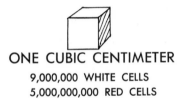

ONE CUBIC CENTIMETER
9,000,000 WHITE CELLS
5,000,000,000 RED CELLS

PENNY

The little box in the illustration, alongside the penny, is a cubic centimeter. If this box were filled with blood, it would contain about 9 million white corpuscles—many more white cells than there are people in New York city. It would contain about 5 billion red corpuscles—more than twice as many cells as there are people in the world.

The red cells are little bags containing a material called hemoglobin, which is bright red. It is the stuff that gives blood its characteristic color. Its function is to carry oxygen to all parts of the body and to carry away waste carbon dioxide and other materials that would poison us if they were allowed to remain in our system.

The white corpuscles are the defenders of the body. They rush to any place where bacteria enter the blood stream and they do battle with the invaders.

In addition to these two kinds of corpuscles, the blood carries the material from which a clot can be formed. This stops us from bleeding to death by plugging the "leak in the dike." Materials that make us immune to a number of diseases are also in the blood. And some people carry protozoa and other microorganisms in their blood.

The doctor can tell many things about the condition of the body if he can get a tiny drop of blood. The sample is treated with special stains. He can set up a droplet on a device that allows him to get an actual count of the number of red and white cells. An R.B.C. and a W.B.C. —red blood count and white blood count—are frequently bits of evidence that he uses in his diagnosis of an illness. He can use blood samples, too, to follow the response of your body to the treatment he has prescribed.

Let's see what your blood looks like. Sterilize a needle with a match. Scrub the forefinger on your left hand with alcohol-soaked cotton. Scrub the finger briskly. Many bacteria on the skin can be removed no other way. If you puncture your skin through a film of these bacteria, they may be carried into your system and will cause a slight infection.

Hold the forefinger tightly between your thumb and second finger. This will tend to squeeze blood toward the finger tip. Hold the needle near the point but do not touch the point. Give a quick jab of the needle into your finger. It will hurt only slightly. Keep squeezing the

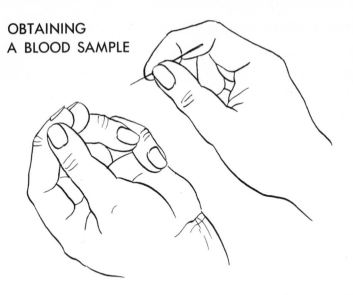

OBTAINING
A BLOOD SAMPLE

finger. This helps to keep it from hurting and also wells up a good-sized drop of blood.

Touch a clean slide near one end to the drop of blood. Use a second slide and make a smear as described for the India ink preparation in the chapter on staining. The blood will spread so thin that at first you may think there is no smear at all. In fact, practicing first with India ink gives you skill so you can make several slides of blood at once without having to jab yourself a second time.

Examine the slide just as it is under low power. The red cells look only slightly pink. Each cell contributes a very little to the total redness of a drop of blood. But there are many thousands of them, as the microscope will reveal. A lack of red cells or the presence of red cells carrying too little hemoglobin is a condition called anemia. The microscope aids the doctor in spotting this disorder.

You will find some white cells in the film too. These really have no color. They are larger than the red cells, and there is only 1 white cell for every 400 or 500 reds, so you may have to search through several fields to find them. If you have looked at other body cells, you will be surprised to find that red cells have no nuclei. The white cells do, though. To see these nuclei, you must use a special stain, mentioned in the last chapter. It is these stained nuclei that give the doctor a great deal of his information. For instance, as soon as a bacterial in-

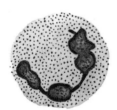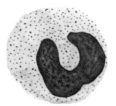

TYPES OF WHITE BLOOD CELLS

A MODEL RED BLOOD CELL

fection sets in, the body begins to manufacture more white cells. A high W.B.C. may indicate that we have a bug of some sort and that the body is at work attempting to overcome it. The type of white cell that the doctor finds in greater than usual quantity tells him frequently what parts of the body are infected.

Students always have great fun with the names of the types of white cells. One of the cells probably has the longest name of any object of such a tiny size. *Leuco* means "white" in Greek and *cytos* means "cell." The white cells are called leucocytes. But white cells have nuclei which are of many shapes. *Poly* means "many." *Morphos* means "form." One particular sort of white cell has little granules in it which stain with eosin so that they show up red on the slide. *Philos* means "loving" or "having an attraction for." The cell is therefore called an eosinophilic polymorphonucleated leucocyte.

If you have high power you can get a good glimpse of a single red cell. Note that it looks like a flat disc with a hollow on each side. You could make a model of one by taking a ball of modeling clay the size of a marble and pressing from two sides between your thumb and finger. Sometimes the slide will show several red cells stacked up like coins in a pile.

If you put a drop of fountain pen ink diluted with

water on the slide and then add a cover glass you will stain the cells slightly. They will be colored enough to show that the white cells have polymorphonuclear structure. Sometimes the nucleus is a single round ball which nearly fills the cell. Sometimes the bits of irregular nuclear material are held together by tiny threads.

We have been told that blood circulates in the system. The pulse and heart beat are only indirect evidence, however, that the phenomenon is taking place. Let's look at blood cells actually tumbling along through the vessels. You will need a goldfish or a small frog. You will not hurt the animal at all and you can return him to the water in fine condition after he has provided you with an exciting adventure.

The job is easiest to do if you make a fish board—or a frog board, as the case may be. Get a piece of thin wood, about 2 by 3 inches. A shingle will do. Cut a hole about ½ inch in diameter near one end. Thoroughly soak in water a piece of cloth or absorbent cotton about 4 inches by 12 inches. The water should be room temperature. Roll the fish in the wet cloth or cotton, with the tail exposed, and hold it on the board with thumbtacks along the edge of the cloth—not the fish. Place the tail over the opening in the board and secure it by placing two tacks along its outer edge. Pin the tacks into the board—

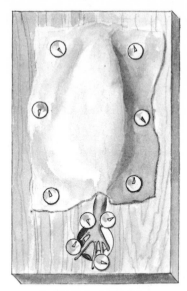

A FISH BOARD A FROG BOARD

not the fish. You can hold the tail in place with very little pressure from the rims of the tacks.

Pour a little water on the head of the fish every couple of minutes. Examine the tail under the microscope. The larger blood vessels run parallel to the rays of the tail fin. Between the larger vessels you will see a maze of numerous thinner branches. These are the capillaries. You will see the blood cells moving along the main vessels from the heart and fanning out into the capillary bed.

You can follow the capillaries along until they reach

108

another larger vessel which transports them the other way back to the heart. You should keep the tail wet all the time you examine it. Drop water from your fingers on it from time to time. It will not hurt the fish if you keep him out of water as long as 20 minutes if you use care to keep him wet all the time. It is probably safer, though, to limit your first observations to 5 or 10 minutes at the most.

If you use a frog, wrap one leg and the body in the cloth to keep the frog from jumping and stretch out the other leg so the web of the foot is over the hole. You don't have to worry about keeping the frog wet. The web is very thin and blood cells may be seen through the walls of the blood vessels more easily than they can in the fish. You will notice that all frog and fish blood cells have nuclei, which makes them differ from mammal blood cells.

When you return the fish to water, watch to see if he swims away at once. If he appears to be sluggish, it is well to hold him by the tail and dip him several times in and out of the water. This helps add air to the water near the gills and he is soon his old fishy self again.

Perhaps you have heard about different human blood types but you do not understand what they mean. Cer-

tain chemicals in the blood cause the blood to be classi-
fied into four groups: A, B, AB, and O. If a person needs
a transfusion, he cannot be given blood from just any
donor, for certain type combinations will cause death.

If you are AB, you can receive blood safely from almost anyone. If your blood is type O, you are a universal
donor: you can give blood safely to almost everyone.
However, you can receive only from O-type people. If
you are A type you can receive from A or O, and if you
are B you can receive only from B or O.

If types that do not combine are mixed together, the
red cells cluster. These lumps prevent the free passage
of blood through the capillaries and so the condition is
fatal.

It is frequently desirable to give whole-blood trans-
fusions. This can be done safely only when the types are
known. Today the red cells are frequently removed from
the blood and only the remaining plasma (clear liquid) is
given to the patient. When blood is handled in this manner there is no danger of clotting.

The study of the blood (hematology) is one to which
many scientists have devoted their lives. As we have
seen, the blood carries chemicals that the body needs, it
transports digested food, carries away waste products,
contains antibodies that fight specific diseases, contains

white cells that fight infection. It is indeed a vital fluid.

Even though much detailed study has been made of the blood, many unanswered questions remain.

We still do not fully understand blood coagulation, which is related to typing; the process by which the body replaces red and white cells has not been completely explained; and the relationship between blood cells and diseases of the body has not been fully clarified.

There is indeed much for man to learn about the blood. Perhaps you will be able to contribute information that will help unravel some of the many problems.

CHAPTER THIRTEEN

Radioactivity and the Microscope

THE MICROSCOPE has become an indispensable tool in all areas of scientific research. Nucleonics, the study of the nuclei of atoms, is no exception. This chapter will show how radioactivity, one of the phenomena exhibited by certain atoms, is better understood because of the microscope.

A substance is radioactive when it gives off particles and energy spontaneously: with no influence from outside itself. Sometimes the particles given off by such atoms are relatively large and massive, in which case they are called alpha particles; or the particles may be relatively light and fast moving, in which case they are called beta particles. Beta are the particles that are most often registered on a Geiger counter because they go right through the glass of the tube.

112

Alpha particles move about 10,000 miles a second but they are quickly stopped by a few inches of air or even a thin piece of paper. Beta particles approach the speed of light, are much smaller than alphas, and, hence, can penetrate matter more deeply before they are brought to rest. Alpha particles are actually the nuclei of helium atoms. They pick up electrons from the surrounding air and are transformed into helium gas atoms quite quickly.

Alpha particles cause luminous watch dials to light up, so if you are wearing such a watch, several billion alpha particles are being emitted in your immediate vicinity. Not many of them ever get into you, however, even if you are wearing a wrist watch with a luminous dial. The watch absorbs most of them. Under the crystal of your watch you would find quite a high concentration of helium gas, too. This gas is the result of the alpha particles' gaining electrons from the air immediately under the crystal.

A simple way to see the effect of alpha particles is to place a luminous watch on the stage of your microscope. It is best to have the watch stopped because you will find that the hands are invariably coated with the radio-active material which you want to investigate. If the watch is running, you have a troublesome time trying to keep focused on the moving hands. Focus under low power in a dark room, the darker the better. It will take you fifteen minutes or so to allow your eye to become accustomed to the darkness. Don't try to see anything through the microscope until your eye is well rested. When your eye is prepared for viewing, you will see hundreds of tiny flashes, or scintillations. *Scintilla* in Latin means "spark." The luminous paint on your watch contains a radium salt or, more commonly, a thorium compound thoroughly mixed with phosphorescent zinc sulfide. Each flash indicates that a radium or thorium atom has given off an alpha particle. When one of these particles strikes the zinc sulfide, light is produced for just an instant at that point.

Radioactive material is quite expensive, yet the amount on your watch dial is only about twelve cents' worth. Nevertheless, radium compounds give out so many alpha particles every instant that this tiny, tiny amount is enough to light up the hands of the watch brightly. A single gram of radium gives out nearly 40 *billion* alpha particles every second. The flashes appear in a random fashion. You can never tell where the next one is likely to come from. It is all a matter of chance. Sometimes you will see several scintillations at one time in the field. Again you may have to wait an instant before any appear. The zinc sulfide under bombardment by the tiny alpha bullets has been described as looking like illuminated splashes rising from a dark pool. It is an exciting view.

If your watch is inexpensive, you may see no scintillations, even though the hands are luminous. This is because the paint contains no radioactive material. The illumination is produced differently from that on a radioactive lighted face. The material used in the paint in this type of dial is called a phosphorescent substance. It has the ability to store up light when exposed to a source of illumination and then to give the light out more slowly after the exciting energy has been removed. Such a material stores up light during the day and gives it out at night. Sometimes these clocks and watches are not very noticeably luminous by early morning but you are asleep by then so it will never make any difference to you. A radioactive dial will remain just as brightly lighted at the end of the night as it was at the beginning.

You can see the effect of alpha particles better if you scrape some of the paint from a luminous clock face and make a slide out of it. Use an old clock whose hands can be sacrificed to scientific investigation. Sometimes your local watch repairman has old radioactive watch or clock hands he will give you. Scrape some of the paint from the hands. Remember that some clocks do not have luminous paint on the numerals. Mix the scrapings with a pinch or two of phosphorescent zinc sulfide. This kind of zinc sulfide can be obtained at a science supply house, or perhaps your science teacher can supply a small amount from his stock of chemicals. Put a cover glass over the mixture of paint and zinc sulfide and fasten it on with a bit of Canada balsam. When the slide is viewed under low power, the flashes will be more noticeable than those from the hands alone. You have concentrated the radioactive material. Even though the amount of radioactive material in the luminous mixture is small and completely harmless, it is wise to take every precaution when working with radioactive materials in any quantity. Wash your hands thoroughly after making this slide.

Scintillations from radioactive particles are so readily seen that scientists have devised ways of counting them and hence have acquired a great deal of information about how radium and other similar elements break down. The first counts were made at the microscope. Scientists spent countless long hours counting each little flash and then calculating the rate of breakdown. At the present time devices are available which use photoelectric cells instead of the human eye and automatic counting equipment instead of the human mind. More data can be accumulated by these and the machines are inclined to be more accurate than human investigators.

They have the added advantage of never getting tired or having to stop for a snack!

The microscope has helped men in the study of nuclei of atoms in other ways also. The 'scope is used in studying the effects of radioactivity on cells of both plants and animals. In this way information concerning the utilization of food by plants and animals can be determined. In nucleonics, as in all other branches of scientific research, the microscope is a tool of many uses.

CHAPTER FOURTEEN

Observing Bacteria

ONE OF the most valuable applications of the microscope is the observation of bacteria. Bacteria are tiny plants. There are hundreds of forms. Some few cause disease. Many more of them are of use to us in such widely different ways as making cheese, curing leather, treating sewage, and fertilizing soil. They are everywhere. They are found in the depths of the ocean, at the polar icecap, and high in the stratosphere.

Brush your hand across the table top. In the tiny amount of dust you pick up are swarms of bacteria and other microorganisms. Scrape your teeth with a toothpick. In the mixture of saliva and tartar that you pick up will be further swarms. Unfortunately most of the kinds that you can pick up readily are too small to be seen well with the small microscope you are likely to own. Bacteria are so interesting though that we should

118

try to see whatever we can see of them with the equipment we have.

Like most plants, bacteria need water in order to live. Many of them will die when no water is available. This is why drying of meats and fruits is such a good way to preserve them. A ripe peach will soon be the home of myriads of bacteria. It will decay. A dried peach gives the bacteria no foothold. It can be kept edible for a long time.

It is natural then to look to water as a collecting ground. Your tap water probably has been treated with chlorine for the specific purpose of killing bacteria, so there is little use in trying it. For this reason, too, it is best to use distilled water, rather than tap water, to dilute fluids that you suspect contain bacteria. Any stagnant pond or puddle, though, is likely to have some. Put a drop of pond water on a slide. Drop on a cover slip and look carefully at the film of water with your microscope. Most people don't look at a specimen long enough to spot the bacteria even if some are there. After you have looked at the water drop a little while, you will notice that the whole background appears to quiver. This motion is due to tiny suspended particles—some of them bacteria— which are being knocked around by the constantly moving molecules of water.

The motion of tiny particles in suspension is called Brownian movement. It was named for a botanist named Brown who made a careful study of it. All bacteria share in this motion. But some of them can move by themselves. If you have collected any of this type, you will know it by watching one individual speck. If it is moving in a straight line a distance of as much as three or four times its own length, it is propelling itself. We call such bacteria motile.

Try a tiny drop of sour milk or buttermilk on a slide. Mix it with a drop or two of water if it is too thick to see through. Look carefully at the clear spaces between the clumps that you see. Focus the instrument very slowly up and down through a small range. The lighting is important. Adjust the mirror in different positions. If this doesn't give a good light, turn the mirror away from the stage and use a light from above or from the side. Don't think that you are seeing motility if all the particles are drifting in one direction. This happens if the stage is tipped. The bacteria are all flowing downhill.

Carefully scrape your teeth near the gums with a toothpick. Puddle the end of the pick around in a drop of water on a slide. You will always find bacteria in the gum margin. The slide will have a collection of clumps, which are particles of food. You will also find some flat, irregularly shaped plates. These are cells from your gum. Look in the spaces between these larger pieces for tiny rod-shaped objects. Stay at the microscope long enough to get the light right and to accustom your eye to the field.

Water in which cut flowers have stood is always a source of bacteria. Don't be misled by the larger moving animals you see. These are ciliata (infusoria) and are much larger than the bacteria you are seeking. They move much faster too. The scum that coats the stems of the flowers is a fine camping ground for bacteria.

To get a better collection of bacteria, grow some in pond water. Use a large jar for the water. Throw into it a half dozen or more dead flies or dead bees. Keep the jar in a fairly warm place in semidarkness. The insects will become covered with a fuzzy coating after a few days. This is a mold which was considered in another chapter. The scum at the top of the jar or the material in the bottom will have motile rods which are large enough to show up well with your microscope. There are many kinds of bacteria that have this rod form. Such a rod is called a bacillus.

One form of bacillus that is of great value to us is found growing on the roots of white clover plants on lawns. It is found, too, on the roots of red and sweet clover, alfalfa, vetch, and soybeans. Dig up one of these

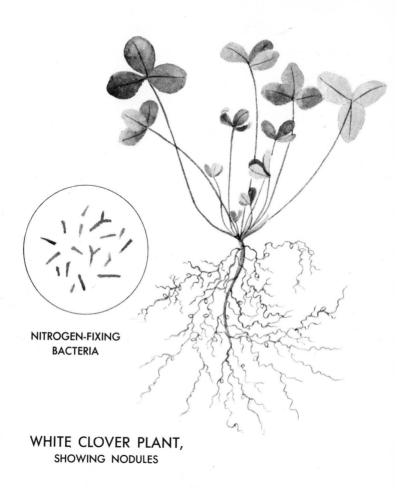

NITROGEN-FIXING
BACTERIA

WHITE CLOVER PLANT,
SHOWING NODULES

plants. Dunk the roots up and down carefully in a container of water to wash away the soil. You will find little lumps called nodules on the roots, similar to those in the illustration.

Select a large nodule. Place it on the slide and crush it

122

with a needle. Smear the crushed nodule around on the slide. Add a drop of distilled water and observe with the highest power lens you have. Look for the bacteria in the thin places in the slide. There will be too many of them in the center of the slide probably. It will be impossible to concentrate on a few single ones. The whole field will look grainy like sand because of the millions of bacteria you will have squeezed out of the single, tiny nodule.

The organisms from the clover root are sometimes shaped like rods, sometimes like clubs, and sometimes Y-shaped. They are nitrogen-fixing bacteria. They are able to take nitrogen gas from the air and combine it with water to form a compound which the plants can use to grow on. The air nitrogen cannot be used by plants or animals. But nitrogen is necessary in our foods in order to produce new tissue in our bodies and to repair the old worn-out tissue. Animals, including ourselves, eat the plants and obtain their supply of usable nitrogen that way. Farmers sometimes grow clover or alfalfa on a plot of ground just for the fertilizing effect of these little club and Y-shaped fellows.

A handful of dry hay placed in water for a few days will usually produce myriads of large bacilli called, oddly enough, hay bacillus. These bacteria are perfectly harmless but they look very much like the organisms that cause anthrax, a disease that is frequently fatal to sheep and cows and occasionally to man. One of the authors of this book used to train laboratory technicians. He had a whole "library" of bacteria that were harmless but looked like disease producers. His students could learn to work with these without any danger. Only after they became proficient at working with harmless bacteria were they allowed to handle the really "hot," disease-producing ones. One day a student prepared a slide of hay bacillus. It looked so much like anthrax bacillus that nobody in the laboratory could be sure that it was not. The true test, of course, would have been to try it on an animal to see if it would give the animal anthrax. The whole culture was destroyed and a new tuft of hay put to work to produce a hay bacillus culture that could be depended on. The difference between harmful and safe bacteria cannot always be told by the appearance of the organisms alone. A number of tests have been developed, however, short of "trying it on the dog," for distinguishing harmful bacterial forms from dangerous ones.

If you happen to live near sulfur or iron springs, you have an extremely interesting source of bacteria. Pick up some of the white scum near the sulfur spring. Under the 'scope you will find long filaments filled with tiny granules. These granules are sulfur which the bac-

HAY BACILLUS

SULFUR BACTERIA,
SHOWING GRANULES OF SULFUR

SOME TYPES OF
IRON BACTERIA

teria produce from the hydrogen sulfide gas dissolved in the spring water. It is this hydrogen sulfide gas that gives the water its characteristic odor of rotten eggs. Sulfur deposits in the earth may have been produced by these bacteria. When you consider that some deposits are several miles in area and several feet thick, it gives you an idea of how many of these little duffers have been at work throughout the ages.

The rusty, fluffy masses that float in iron springs are composed of large rods and some spiral-shaped bacteria, called spirilla. Some of our huge deposits of iron may have been made by these bacteria. They live on the dissolved iron salts of the spring and "spit out" tiny, tiny bits of metallic iron.

The very best way to examine living microorganisms

125

is with a "hanging drop." There are some extra-thick microscope slides that have a little well in the center. Another kind has a ground-out hollow in the slide. Either of these is excellent for setting up a hanging drop. You can substitute for these special slides, however, the special washers described in chapter 4. Build up several cardboard washers to make a well ¼ inch or more thick.

Place a clean cover glass on the table before you. Wipe a very little Vaseline all around the rim. Leave as much clear space in the center of the cover as you can. Place a small drop of water containing the bacteria you wish to examine in the center of the cover glass. Turn the slide with the attached washers upside down and place it over the cover slip. Press it down firmly so that the Vaseline will stick the cover glass to the washers. Flip the slide over quickly so the drop does not have time to slip to the edge of the wall and be caught there. You will now have the drop hanging from a ceiling made of the cover glass. Bacteria will frequently congregate near the edge of this drop where the water contacts the cover slip. Since the cover glass is not pressing down on the water, any microorganism in the drop is free to move about.

RIM WITH VASELINE.

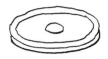

PLACE DROP OF CULTURE
MATERIAL ON COVER SLIP.

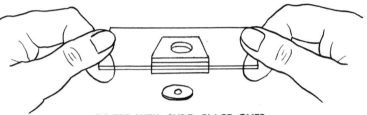

INVERT WELL SLIDE; PLACE OVER
COVER SLIP; PRESS ON SECURELY.

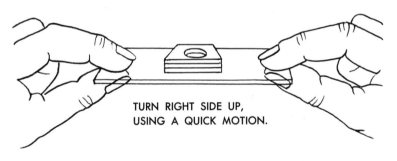

TURN RIGHT SIDE UP,
USING A QUICK MOTION.

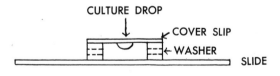

CULTURE DROP

COVER SLIP

WASHER

SLIDE

A COMPLETED HANGING-DROP PREPARATION

THE HANGING DROP

CHAPTER FIFTEEN

Staining

BY THIS time you know some of the problems faced
by the bacteriologist. Bacteria have no color. They are
usually all but transparent, which makes it very difficult
to learn much by examining them. For this reason bacteria are frequently stained or dyed so that they will
show up better. Staining kills them, of course. But much
can be learned nevertheless. Scores of staining materials
have been tried. Some stain one kind of bacteria and not
another. Some turn the interior parts one color and other
parts another color. The techniques of staining bacteria
are among the most important in the bag of tricks of the
microbiologist.

Bacteria that are to be stained are usually "smeared"
on a slide. The thin film you got from the clover nodule
was a smear. If dye were put directly on the smear it

128

would wash off the glass slide. To prevent this, biologists usually "fix" the smear. One way to fix a smear to the slide is to heat the slide gently first to dry out the smear. The slide is then heated quite strongly for a brief instant. This effectively "cooks" the smear and makes it stick to the glass. If you have ever tried to clean a cooking pan that has boiled dry, you know how firmly "fixed" the food particles can be. Dye is placed right on the fixed smear and then washed off with water. The slide is blotted dry and examined.

A common laboratory stain is methylene blue. If you can get some of the dry stain, take as much of it as you can pick up on the tip of a small knife blade. Add it to 100 cubic centimeters—about half a tumblerful—of distilled water. This will make enough stain to last you for a long time.

Eosin is another water-soluble stain which dyes many bacteria red. It can be made up in the same way. Most permanent blue fountain pen ink is colored with methylene blue and almost all red ink is colored with eosin. You can substitute these inks for the usual laboratory stains at least to start off your work. It is a good idea to filter the ink a few times through filter paper or a paper towel. Ink usually has a lot of dust particles, pollen grains, and mold spores in it. If you find this phase of microscope work interesting, you will want to learn to handle other stains.

Prepare a tartar slide from your teeth as you did before, but this time hold the slide high over a candle flame or the flame from an alcohol lamp until the water evaporates. If you hold the slide in your fingers as you do this, you will never overheat the smear. You'll put it down first! When the water has all gone off, pass the slide, smear side up, through the flame three times. One, two, three—no more. This will fix the smear without changing the shape of the bacteria appreciably.

When the slide has cooled, drop ink or made-up stain on the smear with a medicine dropper. Use just enough to cover the smeared spot. Allow it to stand about a minute. Wash off the ink with tap water and *blot* the slide dry carefully. Rubbing the slide will scratch off parts of the smear. Examine it under the microscope. The particular ink or stain you have may need more than one minute to stain the cells well. Experiment with this. Keep a record of the changes you make so that when you find the best procedure you can use it on all subsequent slides.

There are so many kinds of bacteria that it is impossible to tell you which ones will stain blue and which ones red. Try staining all bacteria you encounter. A third common stain—and a good one—is crystal violet. Drug-

1 ADD MATERIAL TO A DROP OF WATER SPREAD OUT INTO A SMEAR.

2 HOLD HIGH OVER FLAME UNTIL WATER EVAPORATES.

3 PASS THROUGH FLAME THREE TIMES TO "FIX" THE SMEAR.

4 DROP STAIN ON FIXED SMEAR.

5 WASH OFF STAIN.

6 CAREFULLY BLOT DRY.

STAINING A SMEAR

stores frequently carry it. It must be dissolved in a little alcohol and then the alcohol solution is diluted with water. Your druggist will surely have gentian violet made up in solution and you can get a small amount from him. This works well, too.

You can use a drop of India ink to prepare what is called a negative stain. This colors the background but leaves the bacteria transparent. Place a drop of India ink on a slide as shown in the illustration. Mix the bacteria with it. Hold this slide firmly on the table. Place the end of another slide on the first one. Hold it at a 60-degree angle. Pull the edge of the slide to the drop. The ink in the drop will spread along the edge of the slide. Now with a slight but firm pressure push the slide held at the same angle to the other end of the flat slide. This will leave a thin, even smear of ink on the flat slide. At least it will if the bottom slide is clean. Unless all the grease has been removed from the bottom slide, the ink will not stick to it. You may have seen the hospital technician prepare blood smears this way. It is another valuable technique to learn.

The India ink smear dries quite quickly. It does not need to be fixed and it can be examined almost at once. The ink is really a suspension of very tiny particles of carbon. They will not let light through. Look for bright

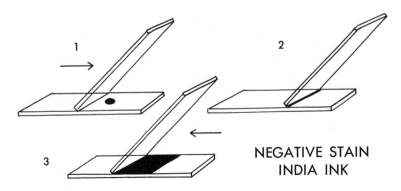

NEGATIVE STAIN
INDIA INK

spots like little islands against a gray background of the ink. These islands are bacteria. The general shape of the bacteria can be observed this way. Look for a bacillus, a rod shape; a coccus, a sphere shape; and a spirillum, a hook or spiral shape. Sometimes these first two occur in chains. They are then called streptobacillus and streptococcus. One kind of streptococcus is the cause of "strep" throat which you have probably heard about. Most of the streptococcus forms you will get to see are harmless.

Cells from your own body will stain with dyes as well as bacterial cells. Your own body cells have the advantage of being larger, too. Scrape the inside of your cheek with the broad end of a toothpick two or three times. Wipe the toothpick on a slide. The cells you scrape off are flat and must not be pushed around on the slide too much or they will curl up. Without fixing the slide, drop on a drop of ink. Place a cover slip on the drop

133

gently and examine the mount. The cells are irregularly shaped but when they are in your cheek they all fit together like tiles on a bathroom floor. Notice that there is a dark spot in the interior of each cell. This is the nucleus. It stains darker than its surroundings. Special stains are frequently used which show up individual parts of the nuclei of cells. The nucleus is such an interesting part of the cell that several nuclear stains have been produced. Try staining with a solution made of a drop of tincture of iodine in several drops of water.

Scrape the palm of your hand with the edge of a knife blade. You will scrape off what looks like dust. Put some of these scrapings on a slide and add a drop of stain. Cover and examine the mount. Notice how these cells resemble those in your cheek. The outer skin cells are constantly dying and drying out. We wash some of them off every day. Our skin, in fact, is like a pad of paper. We take the top "piece of paper" off every day but the pad never gets used up. New cells keep growing from underneath.

Pull apart a tiny piece of beef muscle. Stain this. Now you will see an entirely different kind of body cell. These are long fibers. They have little rings which run around them the short way of the cell. These rings are responsible for the muscles' contracting. A muscle that is under

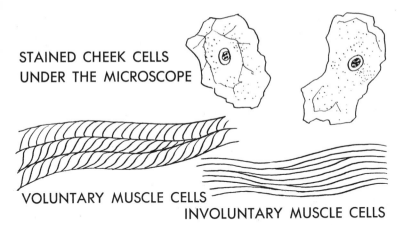

STAINED CHEEK CELLS
UNDER THE MICROSCOPE

VOLUNTARY MUSCLE CELLS

INVOLUNTARY MUSCLE CELLS

our control is called a voluntary tissue. If you get a chance to stain a piece of intestine from a fish that is being cleaned, you will have a specimen of involuntary tissue. You will see that this type of muscle is smooth. It does not have the rings, or stria, at all.

Plant cells will take stain, of course. Bacteria, you remember, are plants. Try staining onion skin and other plant tissues with your dyes, inks, or iodine solution. You will discover a great deal about them this way. If you are looking for a little research project, try other colored inks as stains. Try food coloring to see what effects these have on various materials. The study of stains is almost a science in itself. You have just opened up for yourself an enormously fascinating and valuable facet of work with the microscope.

135

CHAPTER SIXTEEN

Photomicrography

TAKING PICTURES of your specimens is a fine hobby that ties together skill with a microscope and photographic technique. There are endless combinations of cameras and microscopes for taking such photographs; however, many of them are expensive and elaborate. Moderately good results can be obtained with a miniature camera, an ordinary box camera, or for that matter with a homemade device.

The picture shown here was photographed with a small Swiss microscope selling for twenty dollars and a miniature camera. The camera was quite expensive. They were all taken under low power, the enlargement being 50×. First the specimen was placed on the stage and brought to focus. Then the camera was clamped into position and the exposure made.

Now let us see how you can do the same thing with an ordinary box camera. The camera will have to be

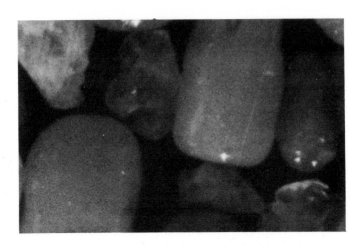

GRAINS OF SAND

placed above the ocular of the microscope in the same position that your eye occupies when focusing. Also a light-tight sleeve must connect the camera to the ocular.

A Brownie Hawkeye camera may be used in the following manner. First, place grains of sand on a slide and bring the object to focus under low power—50× or 100×. The camera is set for bulb, or time if it has that setting, and then balanced on the eyepiece of the 'scope (the flange around the lens supports the camera) and an exposure of 40 seconds is made, using the stage light. (This exposure is made when using Verichrome film. If fast film, such as XX, is used, try an exposure of 20 seconds.) Keep the camera as stationary as possible.

These are some suggestions to help you rig up whatever camera you may have. We cannot be more specific because so many factors are variable, such as the amount of illumination, the density of the specimen, the camera itself, the microscope, and the kind of film being used.

1. Have a light-tight fit between the camera and the 'scope. Make a sleeve from black cloth and fasten it to the microscope with a rubber band.

2. If your camera has a distance setting, place it at infinity.

3. Place the camera the same distance from the ocular that your eye is when focusing.

4. Try different exposure times, starting with 4 seconds, then 6, 8, 10 if you are using fast film. If using Verichrome, start with 8 seconds, then 12, 16, 20.

5. Arrange some way of holding the camera steady while making the exposure. It causes less motion to set the camera in position and then turn on the stage light for the required length of time.

6. Experiment—try different procedures until you find the one best fitted to your equipment.

If you have no camera you can still make photomicrographs. Construct a wooden box 6 inches square and 9 inches long. Cut a round hole in the center of one end just large enough for the eyepiece of the 'scope to fit into it snugly after it is lined with felt or soft cloth. Cut

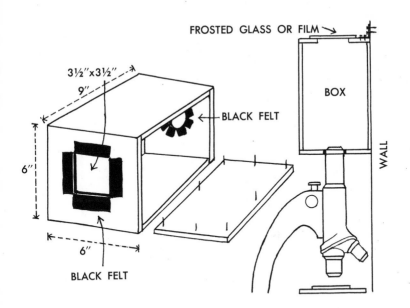

FROSTED GLASS OR FILM

3½"x3½"

9"

BLACK FELT

6"

6"

BLACK FELT

BOX

WALL

out the center of the other end to make an opening 3½ inches square. Cover the wood around this hole with felt or some other soft fabric. Paint the inside of the box dull black to prevent light reflections.

Get a 5 by 5 piece of frosted glass from the hardware store. Or make a piece of frosted glass of that size by placing a bit of valve-grinding compound between two plates and rubbing them together 5 or 10 minutes. You will also need pieces of 4 by 5 cut film from the photo-supply store. (Be sure to keep this in the light-tight container it comes in.)

Place some grains of sand, or whatever you wish to

photograph, on the stage of the microscope and then place the box over the eyepiece. Support the box to keep it from tipping. You can do this by fastening legs to the box or, more simply, by leaning it against a stack of books. Put the frosted glass on the other end of the box. Turn out all lights except the stage light and focus the image on the ground glass. Adjust the light and the specimen so the picture on the glass is contrasty, so there are blacks as well as whites. Turn off all lights—except a red safe lamp—remove the ground glass, and place in that position a piece of the cut film. Make an exposure of 15 seconds if using XX film. These will be test exposures—you will have to experiment before you find the exposure time that is best for your equipment.

Remove the film and develop it, or put it back in the light-tight envelope to take to the photo shop. Mark the envelope with the time of exposure, type of film, date, specimen, and any other pertinent information.

A collection of interesting, unique, and valuable photographs can be made with extremely simple equipment—photos that many professionals would be proud of. Lighting is so sensitive in microscope work that an endless number of variations is possible. We hope you try making photomicrographs, for this can become a most engrossing hobby all by itself.

CHAPTER SEVENTEEN

Some More Possibilities

1. Those odd ropelike things that sometimes cross the lighted field as you look into the microscope happen to everybody. They are due to bits of a fatty substance called cholesterol which float in the outside coating of your eye. When you bend your head to look into the 'scope, they drop down by gravity and appear in the area right in front of the pupil. Notice that, if you roll your eye, they move away. But they come back again. Just try to forget them. There isn't anything you can do about them.

2. If you want to point out things that are under the microscope to someone else, think of the circle of the field as a clock, as we mentioned earlier. A pointer is sometimes handy too. Cut a bristle from a brush. Take out the ocular lens—the one nearest to your eye. Glue the bristle to the bottom rim of the cylinder carrying the

141

lens. Use a drop of household cement or a little balsam. ·
Cut the bristle off so that it extends almost, but not
quite, to the center of the lens. When you want to indicate some interesting thing on the slide to a friend, turn
the lens until the pointer indicates the position of the
particular object.

3. If you don't have a case for your 'scope or are too
lazy to put the instrument back in its case after you
use it, you can cover it with a plastic bag. You can buy
them or, if you watch carefully, one will come to your
house with the groceries some day. They are used to
contain celery and such vegetables. It keeps dust off the
lenses, which is the important thing.

4. Sometimes after you have caught and cared for ·
some microorganisms from a pond, they suddenly seem
to disappear. Stir up the water and look again. Some
rise to the top and some sink to the bottom.

5. Pet shops frequently keep water fleas, called Daphnia, to use as fish food. They can be obtained there
even during the winter months. Daphnia are interesting
creatures. They are transparent enough so that you can
see their entire "internal workings" while they are still
alive. The heart beats, the stomach digests food, the

animals move about. Pet shops often have algae and other water plants too. A trip to such a shop will be rewarding to any microscopist.

6. Hair, feathers, and scales make better permanent mounts if the specimens are first placed in xylol for a few minutes. Lift them out and drain off the excess fluid. Mount immediately in a drop of balsam on a slide in the usual manner.

7. The special stain that colors white-cell nuclei mentioned in the chapter on blood is Wright's stain. It is a combination of methylene blue and eosin but must be mixed very carefully and treated specially as it is prepared. If you can get a small quantity of Wright's stain, the white cells in blood will provide you with a whole winter's work. You will need to consult a book of medical laboratory techniques. Visit your hospital and talk with the laboratory technician about it.

8. We are often lead to believe that all snowflakes are six-sided crystals. However, your microscope enables you to disprove this belief. During a snow storm take your microscope outside to a shed or garage where it is protected from the snow but where it will be chilled to the temperature of the snow.

After a small piece of black velvet has been chilled, catch snowflakes on it. (Since the material is cold, the snowflakes will not melt.)

Slip the velvet with the snowflakes on it under the tube of your microscope.

Under low power you may see six-sided crystals and on the other hand you may not see them. This crystal formation occurs only when conditions of temperature and humidity are just right.

Keep records of your findings. And persist in your investigations until you do find these crystals. They are extremely beautiful and the variety is unending. Once you see them you will be well repaid for all your efforts.

9. Be sure to look for diatoms on the brownish scum found on stones and sticks in flowing streams. They can be secured even in the winter. They are microscopic algae with skeletons of silica, the same material found in sand. They come in fantastic shapes. The material diatomaceous earth is the debris from these tiny plants. It is used as a filler for paper and sometimes as an abrasive in tooth paste and tooth powder. In some places in the United States the skeletal remains of these tiny creatures are many feet thick and must have taken centuries to form.

10. An ordinary bobby pin is an excellent aid in preparing balsam mounts. Simply slip the slide and cover slip between the prongs of the pin and let the balsam set. This will assure an even layer of balsam and bring the cover glass nearer to the specimen.

11. The leaves and other parts of many plants—rhododendron and azalea are two of them—have a very thin skin, or cuticle. Scrape the leaf or stem and you may be able to grasp a small edge of this cuticle, which then strips off easily. Examine it dry or stain it. Petals of geranium have an especially interesting and beautiful cuticle.

12. Some plant cells contain needlelike crystals. Squeeze a rhubarb stem so that a drop of juice falls on a slide. Examine the slide for some of these crystals. The juice of geranium and tulip stems is a source of crystals too. Some plants produce starlike clusters of crystals which are beautiful under the microscope. The crystals are frequently made of oxalic acid compounds which might poison the plant unless they were boxed up in some of the plant cells.

No doubt you have already discovered that the possibilities for microscopic investigation are endless. Everything—oil films, wood grains, paper composition, crystal structures, plant and animal cells—is the hunting ground of the man equipped with a microscope. Many notable discoveries have been made using instruments considerably less powerful than the instrument around which this book is written—one giving enlargements up to 300 diameters. However, the tools available to scientists have improved a great deal, and they have opened entirely new areas of research.

One of these instruments is a three-dimensional microscope in which two images are produced, one for each eye. The viewer sees length, width, and also depth.

Binocular microscopes are also used extensively. In this instrument the operator uses both eyes, but only one image is seen—there is not a three-dimensional effect. By using both eyes simultaneously, the operator sees with greater ease and comfort, permitting him to work at the 'scope longer without tiring.

Microscopes that use light to produce images are limited. They cannot magnify anything that is smaller than the dimensions of a wave length of light. The greater the resolving power of the instrument, the more it is able to separate two particles close together. Under the most favorable conditions an optical microscope can separate two particles even though the actual separation is only 0.00001 millimeter (there are 25 millimeters in an inch). Points closer than this cannot be resolved by a light wave, but they can be separated by an electron microscope.

The electron microscope bends electron beams as the optical microscope bends light. The illustration shows a comparison of the two instruments. Electrons from the source are focused by an electron lens. The beam passes through the object. (Actually the electrons pass around the object. Those which strike the object are impeded

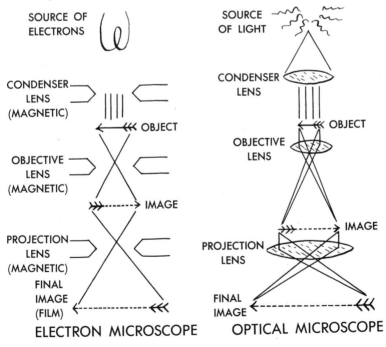

ELECTRON MICROSCOPE   OPTICAL MICROSCOPE

and so a shadow picture is made in the manner that X-ray pictures are produced.) A second magnetic lens produces an image of the object, and a third lens projects the image onto a fluorescent screen, or onto a negative if a permanent picture is desired. All of the apparatus is enclosed in a high vacuum chamber to enable the electrons to move unimpeded.

The picture shows face powder magnified 14,000 times by an electron microscope. It is rough and grainy, quite different from the way it appears to the naked eye or under low power. The structure of bacteria and viruses has been seen under the electron microscope. At this time particles with diameters less than 0.00001 millimeter have been photographed, and perhaps smaller particles will be "seen" when the instrument has been perfected.

Brownian movement, of bacteria, 120
Bubbles, squeezing out of, 32
Budding, of yeast cells, 96
Bullets, scratches on, 25
Buttermilk, bacteria in, 120

Canada balsam, *see* Balsam, Canada
Cancer cells, examination for, 37-38
Canned fruit, mold on, 89
Capillary tubes, 72
Carbon dioxide gas, 37-38
Cardboard, use of, 7
Cardboard washers, 33
Card catalog, filing of, 59, 61-62
Carrot leaves, under microscope, 26
Celery seed, under microscope, 26
Celery "strings," 26, 49, 56-57, 80
Cell division, budding and, 96
Cell structures, preparing, 35
Cell walls, hardening of, 39-40
Cheek cells, 135
Cheese, bacteria in, 118
Cholesterol, in eye, 141
Cloth, manufacture of, 83
Clover, white, 122
Coarse adjustment, 6
Coccus bacteria, 133
Coffee, under microscope, 26
Color fringes, 17-18
Color pictures, dots in, 23

Condenser, substage, 5-6
Corn stem, 50
Corn syrup, in yeast cultures, 94
Cotton, under microscope, 78-79, 81
Cover slips, glass or plastic, 30-31
Crystals, plant, 145
Crystal violet, as laboratory stain, 130-132
Culture, defined, 68
  pure, 72, 77
Culture medium, defined, 72
Cuticle, plant, 145
Cyclonexus annularis, 67
Cyst, protozoan, 65

Dacron, 80
Daphnia, water-flea, 142
Detective work, with microscope, 24
Diatoms, under microscope, 144
Dill pickles, and yeast, 94
Disease, bacteria and, 124
Distance, and apparent size, 9
Distilled water, 68, 119
Ditch water, organisms in, 64
Dollar bill, under microscope, 28-29
Drawings, for records, 60-61
Dry ice, 38

Egg white, under microscope, 26
Electric bulb, filaments of, 25

Electron microscope, 147-148
Enzymes, 94
Eosin, water-soluble stain, 129
Ethyl alcohol, 40
Eyepieces, microscope, 2
Eyes, use of both, 7

Felt and felting, 84
Fermentation, 94
Fibers, comparison of, 81-82
  identification of, 83
  man-made, 80
  properties of, 78
Field of view, 3
Fine adjustment, of microscope, 6
Fish, blood circulation, 107-108
Fish board, 107-109
Fish scales, under microscope, 28
Fission, binary, *see* Binary fission
Fixing specimens, 38-41
Flashlight, as slide illumination, 8
Fleming, Alexander, 58
Flower water, bacteria in, 121
Fly's wing, mounting of, 31
Focal length, difficulty of, 16
Focus point, of lens, 11
Focussing knobs, microscope, 6
Food coloring, as plant-cell stain, 135
Forceps, in mounting, 32
Frog, observation of blood circulation in, 107, 108, 109

"Frozen" sections, human tissue, 38
Fungi, defined, 92

Geiger counter, 112
Glycerine-drop magnifier, 15
Goatsbeard pollen, 98
Greek root words, 92
"Guard" cells, 54, 58

Hair, human, under microscope, 29, 82
  compared with wool, 79
Handkerchief, microscopic study of, 83
Hanging drop, 126-127
Hay bacillus, 123, 125
Hay infusion, 65-68, 74
Helium gas, and alpha particles, 113
Hematology, 110
Hemoglobin, in blood, 102, 105
High-power objective lens, 1-2, 20
Hosiery, knitting of, 84
Human hair, under microscope, 29, 82
  compared with wool, 79
Human tissue, examination of, 37
Hydrogen sulfide gas, 125

Ice crystals, under microscope, 26
India ink, in bean experiment, 51-52
  as "negative" stain, 132
Infusion, defined, 65-68